SCENES FOR STUDENT ACTORS

VOLUME III

SCENES FOR STUDENT ACTORS
VOLUME I

Dramatic Selections from New Plays

EDITED WITH NOTES
BY
FRANCES COSGROVE

Price $1.50

SCENES FOR STUDENT ACTORS
VOLUME II

Dramatic Selections from New Plays

EDITED WITH NOTES
BY
FRANCES COSGROVE

Price $1.50

SCENES FOR STUDENT ACTORS

Dramatic Selections from New Plays

VOLUME III

EDITED WITH NOTES

BY

FRANCES COSGROVE

SAMUEL FRENCH

NEW YORK   LOS ANGELES

SAMUEL FRENCH (CANADA) LTD.   TORONTO

SAMUEL FRENCH LTD.   LONDON

1940

MANUFACTURED IN THE UNITED STATES OF AMERICA
BY THE VAIL-BALLOU PRESS, INC., BINGHAMTON, N. Y.

PREFACE

This volume has been prepared as a result of my discussions with several teachers of the drama. My purpose was to determine what they considered the most important acting problems in order that I might present material which would be of maximum value to the student. Of course, there can never be an agreement among individuals as to what those problems are, but I have selected from the numerous opinions received, those problems which seemed to occur most often.

As it would be impractical to attempt to illustrate each elementary problem by a specific scene, I have consciously chosen a small number of major problems in order that a variety of scenes could be used to illustrate each.

It should be understood that no attempt has been made to solve the problems covered, believing as I do, that the solution is a matter of individual interpretation with the teacher as guide in the question of technique.

Generally speaking, this volume is similar in composition to the two earlier volumes, namely classification of scenes from the best modern plays by number and type of character. In addition I have indicated in so far as possible the type of acting problem each group of scenes illustrates. A series of dots indicates where, of necessity, scenes have been cut. The book list is appended for those who desire to study the play in full.

I wish to thank the publishers and authors represented in this book for their permission to use copyrighted material. I would also like to express my appreciation for the advice and counsel accorded me by Mr. Merlin P. Cosgrove, Mr. Eugene C. Davis of the Glenville High School, Cleveland, Ohio; Miss Elizabeth B. Grimball, director of the New York School of The Theatre; and Mr. Aristide d'Angelo of the American Academy of Dramatic Art.

CONTENTS

SCENES SELECTED TO ILLUSTRATE THE PROBLEM OF:

PAGE

SUSTAINING A THEME

The Devil Passes . . . Benn W. Levy 3
    1 man

The Road to Rome . . Robert E. Sherwood . . . 4
    1 man

White Man . . . . Samson Raphaelson . . . 5
    1 woman

Jealousy . . . . . Eugene Walter 7
    1 woman

Ceiling Zero . . . Frank Wead 10
    2 men

Call It a Day . . . . Dodie Smith 13
    2 women

UTILIZING STAGE PROPS

Michael and Mary . . A. A. Milne 19
    1 man and 1 woman

Touch Wood . . . C. L. Anthony 22
    1 man and 1 woman

Art and Mrs. Bottle . Benn W. Levy 25
    1 man and 1 woman

CREATING A CHARACTER

Winterset . . . . . Maxwell Anderson . . . 31
    1 man

Ethan Frome . . . . Owen Davis and Donald Davis
    from Edith Wharton's novel 33
    1 woman

vii

PAGE

Russet Mantle. . . . Lynn Riggs 37
               1 woman

Blind Alley . . . . James Warwick. 38
               2 men

Fly Away Home . . . Dorothy Bennett and
                             Irving White 41
               2 men

Family Affairs . . . Gertrude Jennings . . . 44
               2 women

Jewel Robbery. . . . Laszlo Fodor adapted by
                           Bertram Bloch 47
               2 women

Hobson's Choice . . . Harold Brighouse 52
           1 man and 1 woman

Spring Song . . . . Bella and Samuel Spewack . 55
           1 man and 1 woman

The Good Fairy . . . Ferenc Molnar, translated and
                    adapted by Jane Hinton. . 58
           1 man and 1 woman

PRESENTING HISTORICAL AND PERIOD SCENES

Parnell . . . . . . Elsie T. Schauffler 63
               1 man

Abraham Lincoln. . . John Drinkwater 65
               1 man

Jayhawker . . . . . Sinclair Lewis and
                          Lloyd Lewis 66
               1 man

Victoria Regina . . . Laurence Housman . . . 67
                 1 woman

Parnell . . . . . . Elsie T. Schauffler 69
               2 men

Brittle Heaven. . . . Vincent York and
                        Frederick Pohl 72
               2 women

PAGE

Lady Precious Stream   . S. I. Hsiung 75
                        2 women

Pride and Prejudice .   . Helen Jerome from
                              Jane Austen's novel 79
              1 man and 1 woman

BUILDING A SCENE TO A CLIMAX

Brute Force   .   .   .   . Jacinto Benavente, English ver-
                              sion by John Garrett Under-
                              hill   85
                        1 man

Searching for the Sun   . Dan Totheroh 86
                        1 woman

Paths of Glory .   .   . Sidney Howard from the novel
                              by Humphrey Cobb .   .   . 88
                        2 men

Men Must Fight .   .   . Reginald Lawrence and
                                          S. K. Lauren 91
              1 man and 1 woman

The Fool .   .   .   .   . Channing Pollock 95
              1 man and 1 woman

SPEAKING IN DIALECT

Let Freedom Ring   .   . Albert Bein from the novel by
                              Grace Lumpkin 101
                        1 man

Stevedore .   .   .   .   . Paul Peters and George Sklar 103
                        1 man

Ned McCobb's Daughter Sidney Howard 104
                        1 woman

Roadside .   .   .   .   . Lynn Riggs 105
                        1 woman

Sun-Up .   .   .   .   . Lula Vollmer 106
              1 man and 1 woman

PAGE

PORTRAYING CHARACTERS IN UNUSUAL SITUATIONS

The First Legion . . . Emmet Lavery 111
1 man

Strange Orchestra . . Rodney Ackland 112
1 woman

Hotel Universe . . . Philip Barry 113
3 men

Children of the Moon . Martin Flavin 118
1 man and 1 woman

Flowers of the Forest . . John Van Druten 122
1 man and 2 women

LIST OF BOOKS 131

SUSTAINING A THEME

THE DEVIL PASSES [1]

by

BENN W. LEVY

COSMO PENNY *is not yet 30 years old. He dresses well and carefully. In person he is amusing and frivolous but in his writing he is heavy and serious. His work appeals to the literati only, and it suffers from a lack of self-confidence. He is a guest at a country houseparty. A game called Truths is being played. It is* COSMO's *turn to tell what it is he wants more than anything else in the world.*

COSMO. (*All his flippancy departed.*) I want clapping hands too: though not for the same reason as Dorothy. I don't want it for its own sake. I want it because I think the position of the Unsuccessful Author is a humiliating one. One is liable to become either what is known as a "disappointed man," a literary hanger-on, or a Micawber. The character of each strikes me as undignified to the point of nightmare. I want success mainly to rid me of my own doubts—doubts about my competence, I mean. My perpetual bogey is that my work is merely tripe, if I only knew it, and that the praises of my friends are merely charity, if I could only see through them. I believe if ever I were completely and permanently convinced that for all these years I have been taking myself with such ludicrous seriousness, but would really have been more suitably, less laughably employed as a respectable insurance broker, I believe then that—from genuine shame, not for effectiveness—I should commit suicide. I quite realize that success is not a final criterion, but it's the most con-

crete and tangible one we have. That's why I want it. That's
the bogey I want to get rid of.

THE ROAD TO ROME [1]

by

Robert E. Sherwood

HANNIBAL *was born in 247 B. C. The son of a Carthaginian
leader, he was brought up with tales of battles ringing in his
ears. When a boy, he was laid on an altar and swore an oath
of undying hatred of Rome. This he never forgot. Physically,* HANNIBAL *is "tall, thin, dark—quiet and surprisingly
unemphatic in his speech—rather diffident in his manner.
. . . He is the sort of man who is apparently none too power-
ful physically, but manages to exist on an inexhaustible sup-
ply of reserve strength. He provides not only the brains
which direct his army, but the vitality which animates it."
He is speaking to the wife of a Roman Senator who has been
caught in his camp on the eve of his entrance into Rome.*

HANNIBAL. Why have I done it? Why have I done what?
(fighting wars, winning battles . . . why?) (*After a moment's pause.*) That's a strange question. . . . I should think
that my reasons would be fairly obvious. I came here to destroy Rome. Isn't that reason enough? . . . Perhaps I can't
explain my actions. . . . That question of yours disturbed me
a little . . . I've asked myself that same thing so many times.
. . . One morning we were camped on the banks of the
Rhone River. It was swollen with the spring floods. I had
to get my army across—eighty thousand infantry, cavalry,
elephants—with all their supplies. We had no boats of our
own; there were no bridges. Across the river, a howling mob
of Gauls was waiting to slaughter us as we landed. From

the south, a large Roman army was advancing to attack us. . . . I sent a small body of men upstream to get across as best they could and to attack the Gauls on their right flank. I was waiting for the signal from that detachment, and wondering whether I should ever set foot on the opposite bank. . . . As I stood there, I asked myself, "Why do I do this? Even if a miracle occurs, and we do cross the river, what then? What will we have gained?" I didn't know. . . . Yes —(we did cross the river) we routed the Gauls, and tricked the Romans, and marched on to the Alps. . . . Have you ever tried to lead an elephant over a snow peak? . . . Our men, who were accustomed to the fierce heat of Africa, had to plod through the Alpine snows, many of them in their bare feet. They had to drag the elephants and all the machinery of war with them, while the natives pushed avalanches down on our heads. . . . When we came to the last line of mountains, and saw Italy spread out before our feet, I asked myself that same question. . . . I've never been able to find an answer. I've watched our men slaughter the Romans in one terrible battle after another. Through all these years, I've seen nothing but death—death—and I've never been able to find an answer.

WHITE MAN [1]

by

SAMSON RAPHAELSON

PANSY WASHINGTON *is a negro girl nearing 30. She is kind, loving and thoughtful. All her life she has known and loved* PAUL, *a young negro architect. Having received a letter from him breaking their engagement, she has come to Paris to see him.*

[1] Copyright, 1935, by Samson Raphaelson.

PANSY. Well! (*Pause.*) Here I am! (PAUL *tries to talk but cannot.*) Aren't you surprised? (PAUL *still doesn't answer. She moves to* PAUL, *laughs at him.*) It's me. Pansy Washington. I came all the way from New York. Don't be afraid of me. I just wanted to see you, that's all. (*Awkwardly—after a silence.*) Well, it was a wonderful trip, dear—just wonderful. I never knew what fun it could be. The water was just like glass, all the time. And all the French stewards—I tried out my French on them. It was funny. Me teaching the little boys in Harlem French and thinking I knew it all—and the stewards didn't understand me! I had to tell them in English. (*There is a pause. She doesn't know what else to say.*) . . . Miss Malone was just wonderful to me. She's the nicest principal I ever had. She gave me three weeks off. Two weeks on the boat and one week in Paris. You should have seen all the other girls—the teachers. They filled my stateroom with flowers. I felt like a prima donna or something. And twenty of the kids were down to say good-bye. It was the cutest thing—twenty little colored kids hollering, "Good-bye, Miss Washington!" (*There is a pause.* PAUL *has not moved. Wistfully.*) Haven't you anything to say to me, Paul? . . . Well . . . I wish I hadn't (come) either. . . . It was hard—getting a letter—a piece of paper. I couldn't just put it down and say, "Well, Paul's out." . . . I had to come. . . . I'm sorry, Paul. . . . I know. . . . It's a woman, Paul. . . . It's a woman . . . another woman, isn't it? . . . (*Slowly.*) You got a crush on another girl. . . . You were in Paris, and you met a girl, and you fell in love with her. . . . And I had to get an inspiration to walk in on you. . . . That wasn't so smart, was it? . . . Me? That's right. I've got to figure out something to do. That's a good question, Paul: What will I do now. . . . I don't know, Paul. But you don't have to worry. That would be too much. I think I'd hate it if you worried. . . . I don't mean to make it hard. Honestly, Paul. I don't mean to . . . I'm not even sorry I came. I can understand better just by looking at you. And I don't think you have to tell me any more. . . . I'm going to stay here for a week. That's what I planned. . . . I guess I'm pretty lucky to get to Paris. How many school teachers get a chance like that? I guess I'll have a lot to tell the girls when I get back. And the kids. I guess a person could stay in Paris two weeks or even a month and find plenty to see. Napoleon's Tomb, the Louvre, all the educational places. I learned all about them on the boat. You go to the American Express Company and they show you everything, and it doesn't cost much, and they explain it to you, too—in English. . . . I guess I'm a pretty lucky girl. If not for you, I might never have thought of coming to Paris. . . . (*She moves to the door.*) We might as well say good-bye. . . . Don't feel so badly, dear. . . . I think it's better that we shouldn't see each other—for a while, anyway. Maybe later, in New York, when you come back to Harlem. . . . I'll be happy. That's my talent—being happy. Don't worry about me. . . . I'm not going to stay awake nights crying for you, so you don't have to stay awake nights fretting about me crying. . . . I don't think I'll see Lucy and Richard. . . . Good-bye, Paul. (*She goes.*)

JEALOUSY [1]

by

EUGENE WALTER

VALERIE *is a young woman, married but a few months to* MAURICE, *an artist. She is the proprietress of a shop. She is devoted to her husband to such a degree that any sacrifice she may be called upon to make, is justified in her eyes by her love. Because of his intense jealousy,* MAURICE *has murdered her old friend and financial backer.* VALERIE *has been questioned at police headquarters. She tells him about it.*

---

[1] Copyright, 1927 (under title *Moniseur Lambertier*), by Louis Verneuil; copyright, 1927 (under title *Satan*), by Louis Verneuil; copyright, 1932, by Samuel French.

VALERIE. First of all, I had to wait a long while. He was questioning other witnesses. . . . He sent for me because I was the last person who saw Lambertier alive before Clement. . . . It has been a terrible day for me, up all last night. Then this blow—and all day down there, looking at the cold eyes of the police—and afraid every moment that the Magistrate might find in my testimony something to arouse his suspicions. You must let me rest, Maurice. You must let me rest—(*He helps her take coat off. She comes to right center and sits.*). . . . Don't trouble yourself about him. Lambertier was a beast. If he was sadistic to us, believe me we were no exceptions to the rule. . . . They told me today that everyone who was near to him was held in some grip with a power which they could not shake off. Clement had at one time made an unfortunate investment, using some of the bank's funds, and while he has paid it back many times over, Lambertier never lost an opportunity to threaten exposure. Jerome told me that he was of gentle birth, and was forced into this servile position through some power that Lambertier exercised over him. He completely cleared me and established the fact that Clement was the last man to see Lambertier alive. . . . They asked me a lot of questions about Clement—what I knew about him, how Lambertier spoke of him, if I knew him personally, my opinion of him. You can readily understand that any number of people in Paris had an obvious motive for this murder. Clement was one of them. He had suffered frightfully at his hands, but he had no opportunity to revenge himself until last night when they were both alone. . . . The police have evidence, not only from Jerome, but from the other servants, that they heard the two men quarrelling. . . . I tried to defend Clement. Jerome and the other servants testified that they had heard the men exchanging bitter words, and a little after twelve, surprised not to hear Lambertier ring for him, Jerome entered the study and found him, as you know, dead. He phoned the police; told them what he knew. Then they questioned Clement as to when he left Lambertier's house, and he answered, shortly after eleven. They asked him where he went after that, and he said, "I went home." They investigated and found that he did not reach there until one o'clock. . . . I don't know (why he lied). But it was that lie which seemed to satisfy the police of his guilt. They asked him where he went after twelve, and he refused to answer. . . . So they held him without bail. . . . But what proof could I give (that he's not guilty. To save him) that was my first impulse, yes. . . . Maurice, will you try to understand? At first I said that I had known Clement, that I had dined with him and Lambertier several times, and that I didn't believe that he was guilty. I was sitting in a chair with both of them directly in front of me, staring at me—staring at me. Then the Magistrate said, "If, as you believe, Clement is not guilty, the hypothetical question must then arise, Madam, that someone else entered Lambertier's home after Clement, and that that person, not Clement, was the murderer." And Maurice, I realized that my honesty and sincerity were turning against you. In a flash I saw you arrested and convicted. Oh, you don't know those men. Their training to pick up the slightest thread. They'd drive and drive, until I'd break. . . . I pretended that I was protecting Clement, because of my dislike for Lambertier. Then I acted as though I was breaking down under the strain and admitted that Clement was of a very violent disposition—and—and apt to do anything when angry— . . . I made up my mind that nothing should happen to you—Clement will have to take care of himself. . . . I said I was in Lambertier's study when Clement was announced, and that Lambertier turned to me and said, "What I have to do will be a sad blow to this man. I'm through with him, and I'll put him where he belongs if it's the last act of my life." . . . I know it sounds terrible, but I was afraid of them, I tell you, Maurice—afraid of them. . . . In some way or other Clement may escape. . . . You're safe, my darling—safe. You've nothing to fear. . . . Listen to me—listen to me. You may be right and feel the need of confessing, of saving Clement. But there is time, plenty of time, and tonight we are both unstrung, nervous. We can't think clearly. For my sake, don't do anything until tomorrow. Then we'll go over it together and see what we really must do. . . . Oh, my dear, in some way it will come out all right. I'm sure of it. We must put this thing out of our minds; think of something else—go on, as if nothing had happened. We must, Maurice—or we'll both go mad.

CEILING ZERO [1]

by

FRANK WEAD

Beginning his career as a war pilot, now 40 years old, JAKE LEE *has risen to Superintendent of the Eastern Division of Federal Air Lines. He is an able executive and his kindliness has endeared him to his men.* EDDIE *is one of his young flyers. He is a smart, likeable boy. Just now he is obviously worried and very nervous. The scene is* JAKE's *office at the Newark Terminal.*

EDDIE. You sent for me, Mr. Lee?

JAKE. Yes, Eddie. Sit down.

EDDIE. Thanks.

JAKE. Did your chute let you down all right?

EDDIE. (*Sits right of desk.*) Shook me up a little, but I'm not hurt.

JAKE. Good.

EDDIE. (*Nervously.*) It wasn't my fault, Jake. Really it wasn't.

JAKE. Yeah? What's the story?

EDDIE. I had to climb into the clouds to get over the mountains. I went to eighteen thousand feet trying to pick up the

[1] Copyright, 1934, 1935, by Frank Wead.

moon, but the clouds were too high. So I kept on, flying blind on the radio beam. Couldn't see anything but my instrument board. Not even the wing tips. Then the Newark beam stopped coming in.

JAKE. That's funny. It was working. The westbound ship had the beam all the way to Cleveland. Your radio was okay. Buzz talked to you just before you went over the side.

EDDIE. Five minutes before. They turned the beam off for a weather broadcast. I couldn't pick it up again.

JAKE. You could have come on by dead reckoning.

EDDIE. I tried that—without the beam I wasn't sure where I was. The meteorologist's dope was no good. It estimated a six thousand foot ceiling all the way. I didn't expect to have to fly blind.

JAKE. Eddie, clouds are apt to shut down on the hills anytime. You know that. The meteorologist can't go along with you and hold your hand. A pilot's got to hope for the best and expect the worst—and handle emergencies as they come to him.

EDDIE. I did that.

JAKE. You picked the wrong way. Looks to me like you had a bad case of pilot and cockpit trouble. You got the jitters flying blind, wandered away from the beam and got lost. You were afraid to come down through the fog for fear of hitting the top of the ridge. Finally you got panicky and bailed out, sixty miles north of the airway, with a fifteen-hundred-foot clear ceiling below the clouds. Now, that's it, isn't it?

EDDIE. (*Miserably*.) I guess that's right. But gee, don't you see, Jake, with fog all around me I couldn't see where I was.

JAKE. Eddie—you had a map, pencil, paper, clock and compass—you could have kept track of your position.

EDDIE. I tried to. But all the time some little voice inside kept saying: "You're just guessing, Eddie. You don't know where you are."

JAKE. Yes, I know. The sky's a mighty big and lonesome place—when it's fogged over. But you've got to use your head—and ignore that little voice. You should have phoned in sooner, too. We didn't know where you were for four hours.

EDDIE. I was trying to find the crash. I—I hated to tell you about it. I'm not afraid, Jake. Really I'm not. I tried to bring the mail through.

JAKE. Eddie—the minute the weather begins to lick a mail pilot instead of him licking it, he's finished. The first time he gets into trouble makes the second time easier. Before long he's getting into trouble when the weather's perfect.

EDDIE. I've tried my best, Jake. You—you aren't going to fire me—just for this once? I know the game. When I was a kid I built model planes. All through school and college I was planning— You won't—you can't do that—

JAKE. Eddie, since the day you were hired here as a rookie, every pilot you've flown with has had to report on you. You've seen the forms we use. One line reads: "Reaction to emergencies." That line might just as well read "Nerve" or "Guts" or whatever you want to call it. Your reports are all excellent—except for that one line. There—on a lot of them —is a question mark. The boys weren't sure you had what it takes. When the time came for you to fly a mail run on your own, I knew we'd find out whether they were right or wrong. We did, last night. It cost us a twenty-five-thousand-dollar airplane. (*Slight pause.*) They've got your final check at the office.

EDDIE. But what'll I tell my friends? They think I'm—good.

JAKE. Tell 'em the truth—or nothing. It's your problem—not theirs. If you stayed here next year you'd be carrying passengers. Suppose you killed a lot of people? You don't want that to happen. Don't be ashamed to take some other job. Aviators aren't heroes. They're in this game because it's a good living and because they like to fly. Maybe you're just not suited to it. That doesn't make you a coward. Hit the ball. Some day you'll have us all envying you.

EDDIE. Give me another chance, Mr. Lee.

JAKE. I'm sorry, Eddie. I wish I could.

EDDIE. (*Rises.*) Well, I guess there isn't anything more to say.

JAKE. That's the works.

EDDIE. You've been darn swell to me, Jake. So long. (*He exits up left.*)

JAKE. So long.

CALL IT A DAY [1]

by

DODIE SMITH (C. L. ANTHONY)

ANN *is 15. She is a sweet, sensitive and eager child. Her chief interest in life is the study of Rossetti.* DOROTHY, *her mother, is a charming and attractive woman of about 40. They live very comfortably in a house on the outskirts of London. It is twilight of a spring day.*

ANN. Hello, darling. (*She gets up and goes to meet her mother.*)

DOROTHY. (*Coming down the stairs.*) Hello, my pet. (*She kisses* ANN.)

ANN. (*Hanging on to her.*) I'm sorry I was cross this morning.

DOROTHY. Were you cross?

ANN. Of course I was. Didn't you notice it? I stalked out in anger.

DOROTHY. So you did. . . .

ANN. Come and sit down.

DOROTHY. Well, just for a minute. I'm rather tired. (*They sit in the two deck-chairs.*)

ANN. Did you have a nice day?

DOROTHY. Pretty fair. I got you a new belt for your white linen. Do you want to see it?

ANN. Not just yet.—How was the matinée?

---

[1] Copyright in U. S. A., 1935, by D. G. Smith.

DOROTHY. Rather a morbid sort of play. There was a clever girl in it.

ANN. Really?—Did you have tea at Fullers?

DOROTHY. No. With Muriel's brother in his rooms.

ANN. Is he nice?

DOROTHY. (*Rather self-conscious.*) Yes—quite. As a matter of fact he's coming here this evening. You'll have to do your lessons in the dining-room.

ANN. Oh, mum—I can't. The beastly gas fire makes popping noises and puts me off.

DOROTHY. You'll have to manage for once.

ANN. (*Heaving a giant sigh.*) Oh dear.—I'm glad you had a nice day.

DOROTHY. Thank you. (*She sits back and closes her eyes.*)

ANN. You haven't asked me what sort of a day I had.

DOROTHY. Haven't I? Let's see. How was the algebra?

ANN. Foul. But it doesn't matter—nothing really matters. Mum, something terribly exciting's happened. (*She sees* DOROTHY's *closed eyes.*) Mum, you're not taking an interest.

DOROTHY. (*Bestirring herself.*) Yes, I am. What was it?

ANN. Well, I saw a picture and I didn't have enough money, so I went for Cath, and before I could borrow it they gave me tea and we talked, and Mr. Francis found I was crazy about Rossetti and he gave me a sketch—not a print—a real, original sketch.

DOROTHY. Mr. Francis gave you one of his sketches?

ANN. Not his—at least, it was his but he hadn't done it. Rossetti had. He knew his father—I mean Rossetti did. And —oh, mummy, I can keep it, can't I?

DOROTHY. Is it very valuable?

ANN. Only to me. At least—well, it may be a little bit valuable. But Mr. Francis said it would be all right. And Mrs. Francis said she'd talk to you. They promised me you wouldn't mind.

DOROTHY. Oh, well, I can't very well be ungracious to them. It's terribly kind of them.

ANN. Then it's all right?

DOROTHY. Yes, I suppose so.

ANN. Phew! That was easier than I expected. You must be jolly tired. (*After a pause, in a small voice.*) There's something else I've got to tell you.

DOROTHY. Yes?

ANN. I had to get the picture home and I'd a lot of school books. I was terribly frightened of damaging it so—I took a taxi.

DOROTHY. Did you have enough money for it?

ANN. I was going to borrow from Cath, but she had to go back for something and there I was.

DOROTHY. What did you do?

ANN. I borrowed from Cook—because the lock of my money-box got stuck.

DOROTHY. I see.

ANN. But, mummy—aren't you angry?

DOROTHY. Because you borrowed from Cook?

ANN. No. Because I took a taxi. You told me I mustn't this morning. Only this wasn't a bit the same—and I was in it before I remembered. You know, when one's excited one does things one's not quite responsible for, doesn't one?

DOROTHY. Yes, I think perhaps one does.

ANN. And then you have to go on with them.

DOROTHY. Yes.

ANN. But I felt terribly guilty. I had to tell you. I'll pay Cook back just as soon as I can get that lock undone.

DOROTHY. You can tell her to put it down to housekeeping, if you like.

ANN. Oh, mummy! (*She flings herself at her mother.*) I think you're the most understanding mother. Will you come and see the picture now?

DOROTHY. In a minute.

ANN. (*Flinging herself back in her chair.*) I feel marvellous now. I don't think I'll ever feel any happier as long as I live. (*They sit quiet for a moment. The light is fading.*) Isn't it peaceful sitting here all friendly? What are you looking at —a star?

DOROTHY. Yes. There—just to the left of the chimney.

ANN. I see it. The first star's awfully lucky, you know. Look, it winked at us. Isn't everything clear and pale? Shelley talks about the pale purple evening—but this isn't purple, is it? It's sort of pearl. Wouldn't it be lovely to be a bird— only it would be an awful nuisance to have to flap your wings. I'd like just to float on a cloud. Do you think days know when they've been specially lovely and exciting things have happened on them? Do you think they feel pleased with themselves? It's funny how some days are all grey and others are all shining. Isn't it nice us being all quiet together here?

DOROTHY. I wouldn't call you exactly quiet.

ANN. I'm quiet inside. Would you excuse me now? I'm just going to write a poem before dinner. (*She runs in through the kitchen.* DOROTHY *sits quietly thinking.*)

UTILIZING STAGE PROPS

MICHAEL AND MARY [1]

by

A. A. MILNE

MICHAEL *and* MARY *are two young people who are very much in love.* MARY *is a pretty girl, quite young, and distinctly middle-class.* MICHAEL, *a potential writer, is the son of a clergyman, intelligent and attractive.* MICHAEL *found* MARY *a year ago, homeless and desperate. Her husband had run away with the little money she had saved, and she was without work. Although he had only £200, he gave her half of it. Since then she has found a job and he has been writing. The scene is* MICHAEL'S *sitting room in a boarding house in Islington. The year is 1906.*

After a slight pause a door below is heard to slam. There is a noise of feet running up the stairs, and MICHAEL *goes and opens the door.* MARY *comes in eagerly, with a teapot in her hand.* MICHAEL *closes the door after her.*

MARY. Well?

MICHAEL. It is well, my child.

MARY. Really, Michael?

MICHAEL. Yes.

MARY. They've taken it?

MICHAEL. Yes. Chapman's taken it and Hall's taken it.

MARY. (*Going down and putting teapot on table.*) Oh, Michael, I *am* glad. Well done! (*Going up to him.*) I knew they would, when we got the letter; didn't you?

MICHAEL. I couldn't quite believe it.

MARY. *I* knew. . . . Happy?

MICHAEL. Frightfully.

MARY. So am I. Now tell me all about it. (*She goes towards the what-not left.*)

MICHAEL. Sure I can't help?

MARY. (*Turning to him.*) No. Talk. (*She indicates the chair left of table.*)

MICHAEL. Well (*Sitting in chair left of table.*), there we all were.

MARY. Who? (*She goes to what-not.*)

MICHAEL. The three of us. Chapman and Hall and me. "Hall," said Chapman, "this is Mr. Rowe." "Mr. Rowe," said Hall, "meet Mr. Chapman." "Chapman and Hall," said I, "know each other."

MARY. (*Crossing below MICHAEL to right of table with two cups and saucers and two plates and knives, which she has taken out of the what-not.*) Hurray! he's going to be silly.

MICHAEL. So we all sat down and talked about the weather. And when we had all agreed about that, and I was agreeing like billy-o the whole time, Chapman said suddenly, "We all liked your book very much, Mr. Rowe."

MARY. Who's "all"? (*She goes above table back to what-not.*)

MICHAEL. Ah! Perhaps he meant Hall. I didn't ask him. I just made a bashful noise, looking more like a codfish than an author, and Hall said, "We haven't had a first novel of more distinct promise since—well, I should hardly like to say, Mr. Rowe."

MARY (*Coming back above MICHAEL to table, with milk-jug and sugar-basin.*) Oh, I *wish* he'd said!

MICHAEL. So did I. I tried to look like a codfish who wished Hall had said since-when-he-hadn't-had-a-first-novel-of-more-distinct-promise-than, but nobody noticed it. Then Chapman burst in again, "If we decide to publish this book, Mr. Rowe, and I say 'if' because there is very little sale for a first novel, however promising—"

MARY. But if nobody's first novel is ever published, then no novel would ever be published at all.

MICHAEL. Just what I said! or rather—what I looked. Because Hall said quickly, "However, I think we can take the risk, eh, Mr. Chapman?" and Chapman said, "In which case, Mr. Cods-Rowe, what was your idea of terms?"

MARY. (*Kneeling down at his feet.*) Oh, Michael! What did you say? A million pounds?

MICHAEL. Yes. I became very firm and business-like. I said, "Well—er—I—er—what did *you* think?" And Hall said suddenly, "Naturally, we shouldn't be able to pay an advance." Very sudden Hall was.

MARY. (*Getting up from her knees.*) Oh, Michael! (*She goes up to what-not.*)

MICHAEL. Then Chapman said to Hall, "I don't think we even paid Dickens an advance on his first book," and I said— (*Rising and going up to chair left center.*)—you must listen to this, Mary, my one bright remark—(MARY *having got cake comes left of* MICHAEL.) I said, "Naturally, as there would be very little sale for it." Pretty good, don't you think, for a codfish?

MARY. (*Crossing to table with cake.*) Michael, how did you dare?

MICHAEL. (*Moving down to the divan.*) There was an awful silence. Nobody knew whether I was being sarcastic or just nervous. (*He sits on the end of the divan, facing* MARY.) I didn't know myself. And then Hall snapped, "Fifty pounds on account of ten per cent. royalty—"

MARY. Fifty pounds.

MICHAEL. —and Chapman said, "If we did this for everyone, Mr. Rowe, we should have to put up our shutters."

MARY. (*Crossing to* MICHAEL.) Fifty pounds! What did you do? Go on your knees and say, "Thank you, kind Mr. Chapman; God bless you, dear Mr. Hall!"

MICHAEL. No, I didn't say anything. But something in my chair suddenly husked out, "Make it a hundred and crash like gentlemen."

MARY. Michael!

MICHAEL. I was so surprised that I fainted. When I came

round, I heard Chapman speak out loud and bold, "Well, well, take a hundred if you must," and Hall said, "And you'd better have fifteen per cent. over five thousand"; and *I* said, "And *you* take the Crystal Palace, dear old Hall, and you, my dear Chapman, can have the St. George's Swimming Baths." And with this mutual exchange of gifts we parted. (*Rising.*) Now who says I'm not a business man?

TOUCH WOOD[1]

by

C. L. ANTHONY

ELIZABETH *is dressed in the best English tweeds by one of the best English tailors. She is quick, intelligent and has a keen sense of humor.* JULIAN *and* ELIZABETH *have met while vacationing on the northwest coast of Scotland.* JULIAN *is "an elegant young man, but his manner is neither effeminate, nor precious. His briskness is, however, a little studied." The scene is the lounge of a small hotel.*

ELIZABETH, *about to sew, knocks her thimble off the sofa and, with a sigh of resignation, gets on her hands and knees.*

JULIAN CHANCE *appears on the staircase.*

JULIAN. (*Leaning over the balusters.*) Playing at bears, dear?

ELIZABETH. It's that swine of a thimble.

JULIAN. Oughtn't you to wear your crawlers? (*He runs downstairs.*) I expect it's under the sofa.

ELIZABETH. I daresay. They do go under things. (*She finds it and returns to sofa.*) I can't think why they don't make square thimbles.

JULIAN. They wouldn't be very comfortable. (*Looking out of the window.*) Gosh, what a wind!

[1] Copyright in U. S. A., 1934, by D. G. Smith.

ELIZABETH. Have you been out today?

JULIAN. No, dear, nor yesterday. For some generations now my family has preferred walking upright.

ELIZABETH. I should have thought you'd have been out on the loch.

JULIAN. Don't be funny, dear; you can't fish in a gale.

ELIZABETH. Not even sea-fishing?

JULIAN. (*He has strolled over to the table by the staircase.*) Who wants to go sea-fishing? (*He opens the sea-fishing record book.*) "Colonel Whistler and party. 140 haddock." What does the chap think he is? The Mac Fisheries? (*He picks up a handful of periodicals.*) You know, the literature at this hotel is positively unique. The *Mission Field,* the *Austin Magazine,* and *Tin.* Just like that—*Tin.* (*He holds out this authentic journal.*)

ELIZABETH. Thanks. I've already digested *Tin.* (*She is studying with intense bewilderment the many spare parts of her sewing.* JULIAN *strolls to the piano and strums.*) Oh, Julian, not that!

JULIAN. You said you liked it.

ELIZABETH. You've played nothing else for days.

JULIAN. I'm sorry but it's important. (*He strikes alternative harmonies and concludes a phrase.*) I'm going to use it at the end of my first act.

ELIZABETH. What for?

JULIAN. Not *for* anything. Just to finish off the act.

ELIZABETH. I should think it'll do that all right.

JULIAN. (*Coming down towards her.*) You see, Sybil stands looking out at the park—a rather blue twilight and the scent of roses—

ELIZABETH. How do you get that over?

JULIAN. Oh, just atmospherically.—Then she strolls to the piano and sings this thing. I wish I could think of the right words for it. You see, she's happy, but she knows it can't last. I want something that expresses the evanescence of life.

ELIZABETH. How about "Here today, gone tomorrow"?

JULIAN. Sounds like a motto for an umbrella. Ah, well, I suppose it'll come. (*He leans over the back of the sofa.*) What are you sewing with, dear, a skewer?

ELIZABETH. It feels a bit like it. . . . (*Her cotton is knotted; she gives a tremendous tug, and the whole line of stitching comes out.*) Blast!

JULIAN. (*Amused.*) Why do you do it?

ELIZABETH. I get hankerings. I see fabulously expensive things, with millions of tucks and things, and I think I'd like some.

JULIAN. Do they ever get finished?

ELIZABETH. No, dear. I wrestle with them till they look like dish-cloths and then go out and buy Celanese.

JULIAN. Dear old Liz. I feel as if I'd known you for years. I took to you that first evening at dinner when you bit the waiter.

ELIZABETH. I wonder why, when there is plenty of room in the windows, waiters always expect you to sit behind the door. (*She pins her sewing to the sofa and sews away from herself.*)

JULIAN. Put your foot on it, dear.—You know, no one who saw you at that would believe you spoke four languages.

ELIZABETH. (*With pins in her mouth.*) I don't very often; I tell people I speak them, and they give me jobs that don't need them.

JULIAN. You're a nice creature. Quite useless to me, of course. Yet I suppose you do exist.

ELIZABETH. That's reassuring.

JULIAN. I mean as a type. But no audience would ever accept you.

ELIZABETH. Why not?

JULIAN. Audiences expect unmarried women of over thirty-five to be vamps or funny old maids.—I say, I suppose you are over thirty-five?

ELIZABETH. Thanks for even the doubt. I'm thirty-eight.

JULIAN. There you are. And your manners are twenty-five and your appearance not much over thirty. A completely mixed type. It'll be years before audiences accept the elderly girl.

ELIZABETH. What a revolting description!

JULIAN. How would you describe yourself?

ELIZABETH. Just as a woman.

JULIAN. Not in a play, dear. . . .

ELIZABETH. Sorry I'm no good as copy.

ART AND MRS. BOTTLE [1]

by

BENN W. LEVY

JUDY BOTTLE *is a very attractive girl—an artist. She is a rather severe type, her general appearance giving an effect of imagination more than style. She believes herself in love with* MAX LIGHTLY. *Her brother,* MICHAEL, *is a truly promising artist but being only 20 years old, he has not done enough to be known at all. The slight stammer that he has is not unattractive. He wears spectacles.* SONIA TIPPET, *with whom* MICHAEL *is in love, is their model. She is very pretty in an undistinguished way. Her speech, overcoming its natural cockney, is a shade too affected.*

MICHAEL *is painting;* JUDY *is drawing. We cannot judge their work, for their easels are turned from us. Of* MISS SONIA TIPPET, *their present model, we have also a restricted vision so long as she too, though nearer to us, presents us with her back. Mounted on a shallow movable little platform, she is sitting very still in a dressing gown of Judy's, her ankles arranged to cross each other, her hands resting on the seat each side of her so that her arms, unbent, form a triangle of*

[1] Copyright, 1929, by Benn Levy; copyright, 1931, by Samuel French.

which her head is apex. . . . Her head is turned full over one shoulder.

For a considerable while they work in silence.

MICHAEL. (*Talking to himself.*) Promising young artist makes a hash of lady's right knee. (*Silence again for some moments.*) Promising young artist m-makes a hash of lady's left knee.

JUDY. Do you mind turning your head just a shade away from me? (*The model does so and, save for the rub of* MICHAEL's *brush on the coarse canvas, there is no more sound.*) . . . Your head, Miss Tippet; do you mind?

SONIA. So sorry. (*Another silence.*)

MICHAEL. F-f-f- (*Then, too preoccupied to make the effort, he gives it up temporarily. At length.*) F-fat-headed young artist ceases to p-promise at all.

SONIA. I don't think I've moved, have I?

MICHAEL. (*After a long pause, her words having reached him merely as an empty echo.*) I don't think I've . . . (*Two slow brush-strokes.*) moved, have I? Moved have I . . . Moved have I. . . .

JUDY. (*As she makes a measurement with one eye closed and her pencil at arm's length.*) I don't know how you can expect to work while you're chattering all the time.

MICHAEL. (*Automatically and without any of his attention.*) Chattering all the . . . all the time.

SONIA. (*Without moving.*) You'd be surprised: quite a lot of artists I sit to do talk like that while they work. (*There is no response.*) You'd be surprised. . . . Mr. Lightly does for one.

MICHAEL. What does Mr. Lightly do for one?

SONIA. Talks and sings for one.

MICHAEL. For one what?

SONIA. For one thing. *You* know.

MICHAEL. (*Still miles away.*) Yes, I know.

JUDY. It's no good talking to Michael; he's not listening to a word you say. Tell me, what's Mr. Lightly like to sit to?

SONIA. Oh, he's perfectly nice really. . . . I never sat to him till a week or two back. (*Again silence for some little while.*)

JUDY. Did he ever happen to mention *us*?

SONIA. Who?

JUDY. Mr. Lightly.

SONIA. I think I did say I'd been working here.

JUDY. What did *he* say?

SONIA. He said your brother was very promising, the most promising painter he knew.

JUDY. Did he? (*She draws on.*) Did he say anything about me?

SONIA. He said something about your being ever so nice-looking.

JUDY. (*Cannot continue even the pretense of working now. Her eyes beaming.*) Were those his exact words?

SONIA. Well, I don't remember his exact words.

JUDY. (*Bubbling over.*) Did he ever tell you how first we met? It was really quite romantic.

SONIA. I don't think he did.

JUDY. I sent him a drawing of mine and asked him to criticize it.

SONIA. It was rather a compliment that he should have done, wasn't it? I expect ever so many people *ask* him to.

MICHAEL. For the first six weeks there was no reply. Then I followed it up with a photograph.

SONIA. One of your sister's pictures?

MICHAEL. No. Of my sister. Then a criticism arrived by return of post.

SONIA. Well now! Did you ever!

JUDY. Michael, that's not fair. You know he explained that he'd been busy. (*Throwing down her pencil.*) Oh, I can't work any more. Let's have tea. Don't you want a rest, Miss Tippet?

SONIA. No, I'm all right for a bit, thanks.

JUDY. Well, I'm going to make tea. (*And she goes off into the little room whence presently we hear the intermittent clatter of cups and the sound of water poured into an empty kettle.* MICHAEL *continues to work in silence; then with sudden impatience he scrabbles his brush destructively all over the canvas.*)

SONIA. Oh, Mr. Bottle! What a shame!

MICHAEL. Go on: you'd better have a rest. I can't work any more either.

CREATING A CHARACTER

WINTERSET [1]

by

Maxwell Anderson

JUDGE GAUNT *is "an elderly, quiet man, well dressed but in clothes that have seen some weather." It was he who was on the bench at a famous murder trial some years ago. Believing the convicted man innocent, a professor has re-awakened interest in the case by inquiring why* GARTH ESDRAS, *a witness of the crime, was not called upon to testify. Doubt of his charge and the enusing scandal have preyed on the* JUDGE *to the extent that his mind is touched. He wanders to New York looking for* GARTH. *Here he meets the dead man's son.*

GAUNT. I know and have known
what bitterness can rise against a court
when it must say, putting aside all weakness,
that a man's to die. I can forgive you that,
for you are your father's son, and you think of him
as a son thinks of his father. Certain laws
seem cruel in their operation; it's necessary
that we be cruel to uphold them. This cruelty
is kindness to those I serve. . . .
Would I have chosen
to rack myself with other men's despairs,
stop my ears, harden my heart, and listen only
to the voice of law and light, if I had hoped
some private gain for serving? In all my years
on the bench of a long-established commonwealth
not once has my decision been in question

[1] Copyright, 1935, by Anderson House.

save in this case. Not once before or since.
For hope of heaven or place on earth, or power
or gold, no man has had my voice, nor will
while I still keep the trust that's laid on me
to sentence and define. . . .
My record's clean. I've kept it so. But suppose
with the best intent, among the myriad tongues
that come to testify, I had missed my way
and followed a perjured tale to a lethal end
till a man was forsworn to death? Could I rest or sleep
while there was doubt of this,
even while there was question in a layman's mind?
For always, night and day,
there lies on my brain like a weight, the admonition:
see truly, let nothing sway you; among all functions
there's but one godlike, to judge. Then see to it
you judge as a god would judge, with clarity,
with truth, with what mercy is found consonant
with order and law. Without law men are beasts,
and it's a judge's task to lift and hold them
above themselves. Let a judge be once mistaken
or step aside for a friend, and a gap is made
in the dykes that hold back anarchy and chaos,
and leave men bond but free. . . .
May you be a judge
sometime, and know in what fear,
through what nights long
in fear, I scanned and verified and compared
the transcripts of the trial. . . .
And still I found no error,
shook not one staple of the bolts that linked
the doer to the deed! Still following on
from step to step, I watched all modern comment,
and saw it centered finally on one fact—
Garth Esdras was not called. This is Garth Esdras,
and you have heard him. Would his deposition
have justified a new trial? . . .

And there I come, myself. If the man were still
in his cell, and waiting, I'd have no faint excuse
for another hearing.

ETHAN FROME [1]

by

OWEN DAVIS AND DONALD DAVIS

From Edith Wharton's novel

ZEENA *is a woman of 32. Having come to* ETHAN'S *farm in
Northern New England to nurse his mother about eight
years ago, she remained after the old lady's death to marry*
ETHAN. *They are desperately, sordidly poor. Even in better
surroundings and with more understanding and love,* ZEENA
*would probably have been dull and humourless. But in this
bleak country, gradually isolating herself from the sparsely
settled village, she has lost interest in everything in life but
her ailments. Whether they are real or imaginary, and no-
one could say which, they are her joys and her sorrows.*

ZEENA. I as't you a dozen times . . . to fix the window in the
spare room. . . . I tried . . . I done my best . . . but I ain't
got the stren'th to do it. (*She glances at him.* . . .) I don't
know what ever I'm goin' to do. . . . I just got to get it
fixed somehow. . . . I tried everythin'—I guess I tried everythin' there is. . . . (ETHAN *slings down his hatchet . . . rises
and runs quickly upstairs . . . we hear him cross the room
overhead quickly.* ZEENA *stops creaking back and forth in her
rocker to listen. . . . We hear him tapping gently at the
window frame. . . . She sighs, goes over to the cupboard
. . . examines a long row of medicine bottles . . . takes one
. . . pours out a spoonful of brown liquid . . . swallows*

it . . . stands licking the spoon thoughtfully . . . as ETHAN
*is heard lowering the window above. Then she puts spoon
and bottle down . . . goes to the stove . . . pours herself
a cup of steaming hot water from the iron tea kettle on the
stove.* ETHAN *comes quickly down the stairs and back into
the room and goes back to work splitting logs . . . without
a word.* ZEENA *carries her thick china cup of hot water over
to the heating stove—sets it down—pushes her rocker close
to the stove . . . sits down, takes up a mail-order catalogue
. . . creaks back and forth . . . sipping and supping and
blowing the hot water . . . sniffling and sighing and having a fine time.* ZEENA *glances at* ETHAN *. . . and then reads
from the catalogue . . . as though she were reading from a
bible in which she had implicit faith.*)

"Energex Vibrator . . . New Type . . . tones up the
system . . . beneficial in the treatment of inflammatory
conditions . . . and all deep-seated complaints . . . twenty-
two ninety-five . . ." (*She lets the catalogue sink down
upon her lap and sighs plaintively.*) I've been awful set on
easin' my pains a mite with one of them things, Ethan. . . .
(ETHAN *is paying no attention . . . she tries again.*) "Beneficial in the treatment of inflammatory conditions and all
deep-seated complaints . . ." (*She lets the catalogue drop
in her lap again.*) I was sayin' . . . I only wish't you'd get
me one of them Energex Vibrators . . . you could get it
all right, Ethan, if you was a mind to . . . and if my complaints ain't deep-seated . . . I don't know what is! . . .
(*With a shake of her head . . . and a glare of disappoint-
ment at* ETHAN; *she fixes the blame . . . where blame is due
. . . according to her.*) Thk-thk— (*She expels her breath in
a long sad sigh—as she speaks.*) Oh, dear— . . . (*After a
moment she drones whiningly.*) The vet says there ain't
nothin' the matter with that cow—except she's starvin' to
death—all she needs is a little feedin' now and again— . . .
(*Continues monotonously without having paid any attention to his defiance.*) That cow's bound to starve long before
pasturin' time . . . anyhow. . . . (*Then with just enough*

determination to win her point.) We'll sell her to Ed Var-
num . . . and get the Energex all right. . . . We might
get's much as thirty, forty dollars if we c'd fat her up a little.
(*But she is suddenly conscious that her argument is in vain
. . .* ETHAN *has paid no attention to her . . . she stops
abruptly . . . glares at him in silence for a moment . . .
then suddenly leans forward in her rocker.*) You ain't been
listenin'— . . . (*She is watching him—supping and wheez-
ing and blowing into her cup of steaming water—she sips
thoughtfully. Drones on.*) It's breezin' in here right now. . . .
(*Sighs sadly.*) The doctor says I won't live if you don't take
better care of me! (*She glances at him and adds pointedly.*)
He asked me again . . . did you see about gettin' somebody
here to help me with the housework. (*She has been carefully
casual and now she stops and watches the effect of this statement . . . but he has paid no attention . . . suddenly she
leans forward in her chair and says impatiently.*) You don't
never answer anythin' I say! . . . Doctor Harmon says to
me—"Mrs. Frome," he says, "you see't Ethan gets you a hired
girl. . . . I don't want you should wear yourself out workin'
around that house—you just can't stand it," he says! . . .
(*She adds decisively.*) Mattie Silver's comin'! . . . (*Inno-
cently.*) She's only comin' to try and help me out. . . . Now,
Ethan—Mattie ain't a hired girl—she's my cousin—she's
comin' all the way up here just to help me in my last sickness— (*She sighs pathetically.*) Besides the poor girl ain't
got any place else to go—you can't turn her out, Ethan—my
own flesh and blood . . . (*Then she adds practically.*) And
bein' my cousin—course we won't have to pay her wages.
. . . (*The cart is heard rounding the house. . . . Nods with
satisfaction.*) I guess Jotham got Denis to bring Mattie's
trunk along in his grocery wagon. Most probably it'd be
about all that old sorrel of yours c'd do to haul Jotham and
Mattie back that far—let alone a trunk. . . . Ethan, the
doctor says I just got to have somebody here— (ETHAN *turns
away abruptly and starts back to work splitting the logs
vehemently.*) All right, Ethan . . . so be it . . . if you won't

sell the cow to get me a Energex Vibrator to relieve my sufferin' a mite and you won't let Mattie Silver . . . my own flesh and blood . . . come here to care for me in my last sickness . . . all right! (ETHAN *drops his hatchet . . . remains stooped over the pile of logs . . . but he glances toward her helplessly . . . she is pleased to see he is weakening.*) I won't be a burden to you much longer—all I ask is you should remember I ain't got a stitch to my name except that old brown merino dress I was married in. It ain't fit to wear, Ethan—so the least you c'n do is to get me somethin' decent to die in! (. . . *She raises her voice slightly.*) You'll be sorry when I die! (. . . *She stops creaking back and forth . . . gazes at him thoughtfully.*) Ethan, you c'n let Mattie stay and do the housework without it costin' you anythin' . . . just the spare room'n three meals a day. . . . Well—the way I'm feelin' now . . . I can't eat anythin' myself to speak of . . . so what she gets'll be the same as my share if I was able to eat proper! . . . Don't fret, Ethan— I'll see't that's all she gets! . . . And I'll see't she earns it! (*She decides that the matter is settled. He has made no further objection so she bubbles along eagerly now.*) Mattie's a real bargain, Ethan . . . course I don't say she's worth anythin' . . . but then she don't cost anythin'! (*She pulls an old brown blanket up over her legs and tucks it in under her and around the rocker and sits back and sighs happily.*) Last letter I got from Aunt Prudence says Mattie's willin' enough but she ain't very handy . . . she was workin' in the shoe mills for a while and she had a job in one of them big department stores down there to Willimantic but it seems she didn't have much gumption cause her health'd keep breakin' down and she'd keep on gettin' fired until now she just can't get a job . . . and none of the family'll give her anythin' but advice ever since her father died leavin' his drug store bankrupt . . . so she just ain't much use to herself—or anybody else. . . . (*The cart creaks to a stop just outside the house.* ZEENA *hastily arranges her blanket . . . dabs at her hair perfunctorily . . . and sighs . . . she*

*feels worse now . . . she sniffles and coughs a little. . . .
There is a discreet knock at the door.* ZEENA, *who has been
poised awaiting* MATTIE'S *entrance . . . relaxes for the moment . . . and cries irritably.*) What's the fool girl want to
stand out there knocking for . . . come in . . . come in!

RUSSET MANTLE [1]

by

LYNN RIGGS

SUSANNA KINCAID, *about 50, is charming, sincere, and seems
to be in a constantly happy haze. Hit by the depression,*
SUSANNA *and her husband buy a farm in New Mexico.* SU-
SANNA *raises chickens. A young poet drifts in looking for
work. The* KINCAIDS *like him immediately and give him
a job. Then they become alarmed that he will fall in love
with their niece. So* SUSANNA *comes out to the barn to have
a chat with him.*

SUSANNA. You see, when I was a young girl, I was the worldly
type myself. . . . Yes, I certainly was. Oh, I've changed, I
know. But *then*— (*She envisions for a second the depths of
her worldliness.*) I fell madly in love with an idealist. He
was so ideal. He built bridges. How he ever got them up
I don't know. He always crossed them before he even started
them. His name was Larry. It was all very romantic. . . .
He wanted me to marry him and go to Spain. Did you ever
hear of anybody wanting to go to Spain— I mean just to go
to Spain? For a trip, yes. But to go over there just to *be*
there. I tried to point out to him that they probably didn't
need any bridges there—they'd had the Moors and all—but
he was determined. It's something I've always noticed about
idealistic men—they're full of determination, and dynamite
can't shake it. I begged him and begged him and he wouldn't

budge. Or rather—*I* wouldn't budge. So *he* budged—and went to Spain. All by himself. . . . Oh, I just stayed in Louisville, and married Horace. It would have been madness to go to Spain and maybe starve to death. Larry hadn't a cent. And I hadn't a thing myself—grandmother was still alive. She was rather weak, but she hung on. . . . Oh, I'm glad she did! It was my salvation. I married Horace. I've never wanted for anything money could buy. Horace is very canny, you know. Sometimes I think he's Scotch. Oh, we've had a splendid life, John! For years, we lived outside Philadelphia. We lived well—yes, magnificently, we entertained lavishly, we helped support the orchestra—you know our orchestra—we made trips abroad— . . . *Never to Spain!* A few years ago we came out here. I persuaded Horace. He had worked so hard. It was time to retire. And here we are—as you see—settled, secure, and very, very happy.

BLIND ALLEY [1]

by

JAMES WARWICK

HAL WILSON *is a renowned criminal. He is 23 and not unattractive though hard and sinister. His childhood was an unhappy one—surrounded by sordidness and penury. Forced to hide for twenty-four hours he has taken over* PROFESSOR SHELBY's *home on Lake Erie. The* PROFESSOR *teaches psychology. Believing it his duty, the* PROFESSOR, *in the short time before him, tries to break* HAL *mentally. A nurse for the* SHELBY *child has attempted to escape.* HAL, *catching her, beat her into unconsciousness. The* PROFESSOR *is a kind, humorous and conventional man with remarkably shrewd eyes.*

WILSON *crosses and punches* SHELBY *in face, then crosses to up of chair left center.*

SHELBY. You had to do that, I suppose.

WILSON. It ain't nothing to what that dame got.

SHELBY. And you had to do it to her too.

WILSON. That should be a lesson to the lot of yer.

SHELBY. Why don't you put the blame where it belongs?

WILSON. (*Turns.*) What? I know where the blame belongs, Mister.

SHELBY. You mean me, of course, but it's not true. You fell down on your job.

WILSON. Aw, you—

SHELBY. If you'd left one of your men in here and he'd let that happen, what would you have done?

WILSON. I'd a plugged him.

SHELBY. Exactly.

WILSON. Sure, nobody— (*Pause.*) This was different. I was— (*Pause.*) I never let nothing like that happen a-fore and I'll take good care it never happens again, Mister.

SHELBY. You think so?

WILSON. Too right I do.

SHELBY. It must happen again and again—unless you find out what causes these rages that suddenly blot everything from your mind. You're scared, Wilson.

WILSON. Scared!! I ain't never bin scared of nothin' in my life, an' I ain't gonner start in now.

SHELBY. That isn't true for a start.

WILSON. (*Steps toward* SHELBY.) Don't call me a liar—I don't take that from no one.

SHELBY. I'm sorry. I didn't—

WILSON. Shut up—and listen ter me. I'm gonner take what I want—as long as I can get away with it. There ain't no other way I can get by now—an' live. Where do you cut inter that picture? (WILSON *crosses to chair left center, then right to left end of davenport.*)

SHELBY. (*Losing his calm for a moment.*) You forced me into it. I didn't ask you to come here—to shoot that boy, beat that girl until she was almost dead— But that's beside the point. You accused me of calling you a liar. Let's stay with that. You made a flat statement that you were not afraid of anything—and I contradicted you.

WILSON. I ain't.

SHELBY. Then tell me something. What are you trying to escape from?

WILSON. What d'yer mean?

SHELBY. You're like a man running down a blind alley in the dark.

WILSON. So what!

SHELBY. What are you going to do when you reach the end? The place where you cannot go any farther.

WILSON. (*Comes down left.*) I'm gonner shoot—an' keep on shootin'! Like I always done. A guy's only got ter get it once—but I won't be alone, don't worry. I'll have lots of company.

SHELBY. You're on the run now. You can't stop to think, can you? You're not going to finish in any blaze of guns and glory. You're going to crack up. You've been on the verge of it for a long time.

WILSON. Crack up? (*Sits on chair at desk left.*)

SHELBY. Yes— (*Pause.*) I'll tell you something about yourself. (*Pause.*) You go along quite calmly as a rule, don't you? See things more or less as they are. (*Pause.*) We'll say, for instance, you're driving a car. There's the road—the different objects you pass—trees—automobiles, houses. And then— (*Pause—he leans forward a little.*) Then sometimes you become aware of another thing you can't see, but can feel. It drives you into going faster and faster, and it follows. You can't shake it off, can you? Your eyes are open but you can't get rid of it. It's always just behind. And presently nothing matters any more—only that thing you feel is there, and you go on and on until—

WILSON. (*Leaping to his feet, knocking chair over.*) It's a lie! Who told you that! (*Pause. Threateningly, as he comes closer and stands above* SHELBY.) Who's bin talkin' about me? It's a lie, I tell yer.

SHELBY. What's a lie? If it's a lie why bother about it? Sit down and don't get excited. It's bad for you.

WILSON. Then yer takes it back?—Say yer was lyin'—go on—say it.

SHELBY. All right, I was lying then.

WILSON. (*Crosses back and picks up chair; places it by desk.*) Whatter yer want ter pull them kinda capers for? That kinda junk don't git yer no place with me. (*Crosses to back of chair left center.*)

SHELBY. No—perhaps not.

WILSON. Say, Doc, tell me something. How did you know that about me?

SHELBY. It's true, isn't it?

WILSON. Yeah, some. Not the way you got it, but near enough.

FLY AWAY HOME [1]

by

DOROTHY BENNETT AND IRVING WHITE

JAMES MASTERS *is a middle-aged man who has traveled a good deal in his capacity of engineer. He is a man's man—hearty and genial.* GABRIEL *is a young Portuguese. He is huge. Usually indolent and easy-going, he is in this scene quite the reverse. He has come to the Master's cottage on Cape Cod to beat up* JAMES's *son for flirting with his sweetheart.* JAMES *intercepts.*

JAMES. (*Very, very cordially.*) So you're Gabriel, hey?

GABRIEL. Yeah.

JAMES. I've heard a lot about you.

GABRIEL. About me?

JAMES. Sure, Corey thinks you're a swell fellow.

GABRIEL. Corey thinks I'm swell fellow—hah!

JAMES. (*Is gradually getting* GABRIEL *away from left door.*) Yes, they all do. They think you're the greatest fisherman in the world.

GABRIEL. Oh, that! Sure. Say, listen, I want—

JAMES. You know, Gabriel, if you hadn't come here looking for me today I'd have gone looking for you. Here, sit down.

GABRIEL. (*Sitting on the sofa awkwardly.*) Looking for me? What for?

JAMES. Because I'm lonesome. I haven't had a real talk with a man since I've been here. Boys—yes—Corey and Johnny. But that's not like sitting down with a man and having a smoke and a talk. Here, try one of these! (*Gives* GABRIEL *a cigarette.*)

GABRIEL. Say, listen, I want—

JAMES. Here, let me give you a light!

GABRIEL. Oh, yes—sure!

JAMES. I suppose you're going out on the fishing grounds tonight.

GABRIEL. Tonight? We don't go out on fishing grounds to-night.

JAMES. No?

GABRIEL. No, it's going to storm. Don't go fishing in storm.

JAMES. That just goes to show you how much I know about fishing.

GABRIEL. You don't fish, eh?

JAMES. No, farming's my business.

GABRIEL. You a farmer?

JAMES. Used to be.

GABRIEL. (*Thawing.*) That's funny. I'm *going* to be a farmer.

JAMES. No!

GABRIEL. Yeah.

JAMES. Well, now, that's a coincidence. Here we are neighbors. You're going to be a farmer. I used to be a farmer. It only goes to prove what a small world it is after all.

GABRIEL. (*Smiling.*) Sure, sure, that's right! What kind of farm?

JAMES. Chicken.

GABRIEL. (*Smiling.*) That's funny. That's *very* funny.

JAMES. You too? (GABRIEL *nods.*) Well, what do you know about that? Just you and the wife, eh?

GABRIEL. No, I'm not married. But I'm going to be married. (*Remembers what he came for and suddenly scowls, pounds the edge of the sofa with his open hand and stands up.*) Hey! Where's Corey? I wanta see Corey.

JAMES. (*Getting up too.*) We'll call Corey in a minute. But about this farm business. You're engaged, eh?

GABRIEL. Yeah, Maria.

JAMES. Maria?

GABRIEL. Yeah, Maria—you know.

JAMES. Oh—not that beautiful girl?

GABRIEL. (*Still frowning.*) Maria. She brings the eggs.

JAMES. Gabriel, I congratulate you. That's wonderful. You know, I like that. I like to see young people have enterprise. I like to see them happy. Gabriel, you'll succeed. I know it. So you're going to have a little place in the country all your own—just you and Maria— Say, what are you waiting for? Why don't you get married right away?

GABRIEL. Well, Maria, she says wait.

JAMES. Wait? What for?

GABRIEL. Money. Maria she says—

JAMES. Yes, I see what she means. She wants to start right. Well—

GABRIEL. Yes, that's right, Mr. Masters, but look—I got enough money to get started now. But Maria she says "no, not yet—we must wait—we must wait for the refrigerator."

JAMES. Refrigerator?

GABRIEL. Yes, for the eggs. Electrics. You know, that takes lot of money.

JAMES. Why don't you borrow it?

GABRIEL. Two hundred dollars? Hah!

JAMES. Two hundred dollars? You mean to tell me you're postponing a wedding with a beautiful girl like Maria for two hundred dollars? Gabriel, I'm ashamed of you. I'll fix that. (*Gets out his bill-case.*)

GABRIEL. What you going to do?

JAMES. I'm going to give you a wedding present.

GABRIEL. (*Getting terribly excited.*) You going to give me wedding present— Oh, Mr. Masters, thanks very much—

JAMES. Not a word. We're neighbors, aren't we? This is just a neighborly gesture.

GABRIEL. Oh, thanks, Mr. Masters. Thanks very much.

JAMES. Oh, not at all!

GABRIEL. (*Taking money, almost hysterically excited.*) Oh, I'm going to show Maria. Thank you, Mr. Masters— (*Starts for right center door, but rushes back to shake hands with* JAMES.)

JAMES. Just a minute. Didn't you want to see Corey?

GABRIEL. Corey? No, I see him some other time. I'm going to go now tell Maria. Good night, Mr. Masters—

JAMES. Good night.

FAMILY AFFAIRS [1]

by

GERTRUDE JENNINGS

LADY MADEHURST, *at 75, is still a very beautiful and charming woman and knows it. "She moves slowly, for indeed she has an occasional 'twinge' of rheumatism, though she never admits it. When it comes to talking, however, she can get in as many words to the minute as any woman."* AMY WIGMORE *is* LADY MADEHURST'S *sister and ten years her junior. They are extremely fond of each other.* "AMY *is just a little*

[1] Copyright, 1934, by Gertrude Jennings.

bit silly . . . small and wizened and has thin grey hair. Her
taste in dress is rather unfortunate, as she has a fancy for gay
colours which are not always well matched." LADY MADE-
HURST'S *son,* SYDNEY, *was forced to leave England to avoid*
standing trial for embezzlement. LADY MADEHURST *and* AMY
were told that he died.

Enter AMY, *very flustered, dressed even worse than be-*
fore—another terrible hat of brilliant colours well on one
side of her head.

LADY MADEHURST. Well, Amy, late as usual.

AMY. I couldn't help it, Elizabeth. I've had a terrible shock!

LADY MADEHURST. Your hat is completely over one ear.

AMY. Oh, never mind my hat, Elizabeth! You don't know
what I've seen! . . .

LADY MADEHURST. There's a hole in your stocking, Amy.

AMY. I can't help it. I'm completely breathless.

LADY MADEHURST. That needn't affect your stockings.

AMY. Don't scold me, Elizabeth! I feel quite faint.

LADY MADEHURST. Do you, dear? I am sorry. You had better
sit down. Now, take my salts. Though when we shall get
our drive I really don't know.

AMY. (*Sniffs violently and chokes.*) Thank you. Oh, Elizabeth! I have had a vision.

LADY MADEHURST. I seem to have a vision also! Can it be
possible, Amy, that you have *paint* on your cheeks?

AMY. Of course I haven't, Elizabeth! It's only ashes of roses.

LADY MADEHURST. What is the difference, may I ask?

AMY. Oh, Elizabeth, you talk about paint and stockings
when my heart is bursting! . . .

LADY MADEHURST. Now, Amy.

AMY. (*With great emotion.*) Elizabeth! I have just seen
Sydney!

LADY MADEHURST. Sydney?

AMY. My nephew. Your son. Sydney!

LADY MADEHURST. What are you saying, Amy? Have you
gone completely off your head? Darling Sydney has been

dead for many years! Do you mean my poor Amy, that you think you have seen a ghost? If so, don't come to me with these tales.

AMY. No, Elizabeth, no! Not a ghost. Sydney himself.

LADY MADEHURST. When? Where?

AMY. Just now—at the corner. Going into a public-house.

LADY MADEHURST. Preposterous! You ought to be ashamed of yourself, Amy.

AMY. But, Elizabeth, I *saw* him, I tell you. And then I went and looked over the wire blind, and he was there. He was still there, Elizabeth!

LADY MADEHURST. Of course *some*one was still there! He wouldn't melt! But it wasn't Sydney!

AMY. It was! It was! Of course, he's terribly changed. His hair's white! He's ever so much older! But he's Sydney!

LADY MADEHURST. If you really thought so, why didn't you speak to him?

AMY. Elizabeth! How could I go into a low public-house crowded with rough men! I waited outside for a minute or two, and he kept on drinking and drinking, and at last I thought I'd better come and tell you. So I ran here as fast as I could. Oh dear, oh dear! (*She cries.*)

LADY MADEHURST. (*Taking her to the sofa and petting her.*) Now, Amy, dear, now don't upset yourself. Really you mustn't have these fancies. Try and think how impossible it all is! Sydney alive! Without writing to us for so many years? In London without letting us know! And drinking! Really, Amy!

AMY. I felt so *sure!*

LADY MADEHURST. Yes, yes, I understand. Now wipe your eyes. And do take that stuff off your cheeks. Here's a clean handkerchief. (*Pause.*)

AMY. I think I should like to go and wash my face, Elizabeth.

LADY MADEHURST. A very good idea. Go up to my bedroom.

AMY. (*Rising.*) Yes, Elizabeth.

LADY MADEHURST. Ask Hannah to give you m)
Cologne.
AMY. Yes, Elizabeth. (*Exits.*)

JEWEL ROBBERY [1]

by

LASZLO FODOR

Adapted by Bertram Bloch

TERI *is a romantic though rather skeptical young woman of unusual charm. Married to a very wealthy man who showers on her every luxury she is, nevertheless, very bored. Her husband promises her a beautiful diamond ring which will make her the envy of every woman in Vienna. While purchasing the ring a very gentlemanly robber calmly walks into the shop and packs up all the jewels including her ring. Intrigued by him,* TERI *gives him her word that she will give him time to get away before calling the police if he will leave her unbound.* MARIANNE *is* TERI'S *best friend. She is about 35. Beautiful, flippant, she is not as clever or as daring as* TERI. *The scene is the drawing room in* TERI'S *home a few hours later.*

MARIANNE. (*Center.*) Teri, it would be rather fun to go looking for the robber—or still better, two robbers.
TERI. Aren't we ever going to speak of anything else? It isn't funny any more. (*Sits left.*) My nerves are going to pieces. I've been feeling for the longest time now that someone is watching me.
MARIANNE. What?
TERI. Please look out on the balcony.
MARIANNE. What?

TERI. Can't you look out on the balcony for me? Someone's out there.

MARIANNE. (*Crosses to left center window, then to right center window.*) Well, if it's to do you a favor I'll look out. (MARIANNE *looks carefully through the pane in the right center window.*)

TERI. Well?

MARIANNE. Not a soul there— (*Turns down.*)

TERI. (*Relieved and disappointed.*) Oh, what a relief!

MARIANNE. Oh, yes. What a relief!

TERI. Please be nice to me—

MARIANNE. Then be nice to me. End my suspense. (*Crosses left.*) He wasn't really short and fat, was he?

TERI. He was short and fat.

MARIANNE. Yes, yes, for the Police. But, unofficially, what was he like?

TERI. (*Surrendering.*) Charming.

MARIANNE. Really attractive, then?

TERI. Beyond your dreams.

MARIANNE. With an air?

TERI. He robbed that shop with the manner of an Emperor bestowing a Cross of Honor.

MARIANNE. Marvelous!

TERI. And at the same time so gay—so well poised. You could see he moves in the best circles. A man of culture. As I watched him go about his business so simply, I realized what a high civilization we really have in Europe today. . . . (*Rises.*) Sh! (*Crosses to center.*) Listen!

MARIANNE. What's the matter?

TERI. Someone's walking in the garden.

MARIANNE. Nonsense.

TERI. Someone's walking in the garden. I can hear the gravel crunching.

MARIANNE. . . . I hear it, too.

TERI. Look out the door quickly. (TERI *pulls* MARIANNE *up.*)

MARIANNE. I'm afraid.

TERI. Please, for my sake.

MARIANNE. (*Crosses up right to window.*) Wait. (*She tip-toes nervously to right center window and then starts back.*) . . . A man is walking through the garden. (*Turns.*)

TERI. (*In a rush crosses to right center window.*) Quick, quick let me see.

MARIANNE. There, see, he'll soon pass the arc lamp.

TERI. Heavens! My heart's breaking through my ribs.

MARIANNE. There! He's stepping into the light.

TERI. (*Screams.*) Ah— (*Laughing lightly.* MARIANNE *crosses down center.*) How stupid. That's the chauffeur. (*She turns away and then stops. Looking at the roses on the console table right.*) Where did those roses come from? When I left the house they weren't here. I remember distinctly that vase was empty.

MARIANNE. Someone sent them.

TERI. You are brilliant, but who?

MARIANNE. Your husband.

TERI. You should know better than that.

MARIANNE. Paul.

TERI. He hasn't the imagination to send anything but orchids.

MARIANNE. An unknown admirer?

TERI. Possibly. (*Crosses right.*) There's no card. . . .

MARIANNE. Roses don't fly in windows. (*Crosses.*)

TERI. (*Suddenly.*) Why not?

MARIANNE. What?

TERI. I met someone today who makes a point of flying in windows. Marianne, someone has been in this room. (*She runs to the window left center.*) The balcony door is un-latched!

MARIANNE. (*Sits on couch.*) I'm going to faint.

TERI. (*Upset.*) I felt it from the moment I stepped into the room. . . . My jewelry! My jewelry is in this room!

MARIANNE. Where?

TERI. In the safe. Back of that picture. In the wall. Please look. I'm too frightened.

MARIANNE. (*Removes the picture in front of wall safe down center.*) The safe has been broken open.

TERI. This is the end! He's taken everything! All my beautiful things! . . .

MARIANNE. My poor darling, cry if it will help you!

TERI. Franz was right! I'm a romantic idiot! I hope they catch him and kill him! . . . Making a fool of me, sending me flowers—flowers— (*She reaches into the safe; finds the jewel-case; takes it out; looks at it, and then opens it.*) It's all here.—Not a thing is missing—

MARIANNE. Then why in Heaven—?

TERI. There's more!

MARIANNE. More? More what?

TERI. The ring, the ring he stole from me today.—That's here, too!

MARIANNE. How could it be?

TERI. Look! (*She shows it.*) The sweet thing! He's made me a gift of my ring.

MARIANNE. That would happen to you.

TERI (*Delighted.*) What a sense of humor! Lets people think he's a robber when he's really a philanthropist.

MARIANNE. (*Trying to realize all this.*) I must get hold of myself. (*She drops onto stool left.*)

TERI. I have received a gift—(*Playing with the idea.*)—I have received a gift from a robber. In the midst of danger, with a hundred policemen pursuing him, he brought it.— I'd like to see anyone have a more exciting experience than that.

MARIANNE. But it is all so immoral.

TERI. He is marvelous.

MARIANNE. Teri!

TERI. But now that I have the ring, what am I going to do with it?

MARIANNE. You must telephone the police at once.

TERI. To tell them that I have it?

MARIANNE. Of course.

TERI. Impossible.

MARIANNE. Ah! You admit, then, that you did let him get away?

TERI. Yes. Even if he is a robber to us, he stormed that shop like a hero. Yes, I admit I let him go. (*Crosses away right.*)

MARIANNE. (*Steps after* TERI.) Poor Teri. How will you ever get out of this affair?

TERI. I wish I knew. And the worst of it is, I can't keep the ring though I want it so much. It's sure to be discovered.

MARIANNE. Why, of course.

TERI. I must return the ring to him.

MARIANNE. Are you crazy? A twenty-eight-carat stone?

TERI. I must.

MARIANNE. Yes, but where are you going to find him?

TERI. He'll find me.

MARIANNE. Then please order the car for me at once.

TERI. Marianne! You're leaving me in such a crisis?

MARIANNE. I have been a good audience for you all your life. . . . But this time I won't help you. This is going too far. There's going to be a scandal, and I'm going to protect myself. (*Rings for* MAID.) . .

TERI. Please, please stay here tonight!

MARIANNE. I should say not. And I'm going at once. . . . (MAID *entering right.*)

TERI. See that Madame Horn is taken home in the roadster. Tell the chauffeur. (MAID *exits right.*) . . . I hope you're disgusted with yourself. There, you can go now.

MARIANNE. And I'm going. Be displeased with me. I can't help it. . . . I'm afraid. (*She crosses to the door right.*)

TERI. Do you think I'm not afraid? I hardly dare go to sleep. I shall certainly dream about him. . . . (MARIANNE *exits right.* TERI *looks nervously around and locks first the door right and then the window right center. She feels better. Murmuring.*) Thank Heavens.

HOBSON'S CHOICE [1]

by

HAROLD BRIGHOUSE

The HOBSON'S *are Lancashire people—middle class and proud of it.* MAGGIE *is the eldest of three girls. Being 30 she is considered a spinster, and as she has made herself indispensable to her father in his boot shop, he will not try even to find her a husband.* MAGGIE *is smart and her tongue is sharp.* WILLIE MOSSOP *is about* MAGGIE'S *age, tall and lanky. "He is the raw material of a charming man, but, at present, it requires a very keen eye to detect his potentialities." The year is 1880.*

MAGGIE. Willie, come here. (*In a moment* WILLIE *appears, and stops half-way up.*)

WILLIE. Yes, Miss Maggie?

MAGGIE. Come up, and put the trap down, I want to talk to you. (*He comes reluctantly.*)

WILLIE. We're very busy in the cellar.

MAGGIE. Show me your hands, Willie.

WILLIE. They're dirty. (*He holds them out hesitatingly.*)

MAGGIE. Yes, they're dirty, but they're clever. They can shape the leather like no other man's that ever come into the shop. Who taught you, Willie? (*She retains his hands.*)

WILLIE. Why, Miss Maggie, I learnt my trade here.

MAGGIE. Hobson's never taught you to make boots the way you do.

WILLIE. I've had no other teacher.

MAGGIE. (*Dropping his hands.*) And needed none. You're a natural born genius at making boots. It's a pity you're a natural fool at all else.

WILLIE. I'm not much good at 'owt but leather, and that's a fact.

MAGGIE. When are you going to leave Hobson's?

WILLIE. Leave Hobson's? I—I thought I gave satisfaction.

MAGGIE. Don't you want to leave?

WILLIE. Not me. I've been at Hobson's all my life and I'm not for leaving till I'm made.

MAGGIE. I said you were a fool.

WILLIE. Then I'm a loyal fool.

MAGGIE. Don't you want to get on, Will Mossop? You heard what Mrs. Hepworth said. You know the wages you get and you know the wages a bootmaker like you could get in one of the big shops in Manchester.

WILLIE. Nay, I'd be feared to go in them fine places.

MAGGIE. What keeps you here? Is it the—the people?

WILLIE. I dunno what it is. I'm used to being here.

MAGGIE. Do you know what keeps this business on its legs? Two things: one's the good boots you make that sell themselves, the other's the bad boots other people make and I sell. We're a pair, Will Mossop.

WILLIE. You're a wonder in the shop, Miss Maggie.

MAGGIE. And you're a marvel in the workshop. Well?

WILLIE. Well, what?

MAGGIE. It seems to me to point one way.

WILLIE. What way is that?

MAGGIE. You're leaving me to do the work, my lad.

WILLIE. I'll be getting back to my stool, Miss Maggie.

MAGGIE. You'll go back when I've done with you. I've watched you for a long time and everything I've seen, I've liked. I think you'll do for me.

WILLIE. What way, Miss Maggie?

MAGGIE. Will Mossop, you're my man. Six months I've counted on you and it's got to come out some time.

WILLIE. But I never—

MAGGIE. I know you never, or it 'ud not be left to me to do the job like this.

WILLIE. I'll—I'll sit down. (*He sits, mopping his brow.*) I'm feeling queer-like. What dost want me for?

MAGGIE. To invest in. You're a business proposition in the shape of a man.

WILLIE. I've got no head for business at all.

MAGGIE. But I have. My brain and your hands 'ull make a working partnership.

WILLIE. (*Getting up, relieved.*) Partnership! Oh, that's a different thing. I thought you were axing me to wed you.

MAGGIE. I am.

WILLIE. Well, by gum. And you the master's daughter.

MAGGIE. Maybe that's why, Will Mossop. Maybe I've had enough of father, and you're as different from him as any man I know.

WILLIE. It's a bit awkward-like.

MAGGIE. And you don't help me any, lad. What's awkward about it?

WILLIE. You talking to me like this.

MAGGIE. I'll tell you something, Will. It's a poor sort of woman who'll stay lazy when she sees her best chance slipping from her. A Salford life's too near the bone to lose things through the fear of speaking out.

WILLIE. I'm your best chance?

MAGGIE. You are that, Will.

WILLIE. Well, by gum. I never thought of this.

MAGGIE. Think of it now.

WILLIE. I am doing. Only the blow's a bit too sudden to think very clear. I've a great respect for you, Miss Maggie. You've a shapely body, and you're a masterpiece at selling in the shop, but when it comes to marrying, I'm bound to tell you that I'm none in love with you.

MAGGIE. Wait till you're asked. I want your hand in mine and your word for it that you'll go through life with me for the best we can get out of it.

WILLIE. We'd not get much without there's love between us, lass.

MAGGIE. I've got the love all right.

WILLIE. Well, I've not, and that's honest.

MAGGIE. We'll get along without.

WILLIE. You're kind of set on this. It's a puzzle to me all ways. . . . What makes it so desperate awkward is that I'm tokened.

MAGGIE. You're what?

WILLIE. I'm tokened to Ada Figgins.

MAGGIE. Then you'll loose and quick. . . . I've got my work cut out, but there's the makings of a man about you.

WILLIE. I wish you'd leave me alone.

MAGGIE. So does the fly when the spider catches him. You're my man, Willie Mossop.

WILLIE. Aye, so you say. Ada would tell another story, though.

SPRING SONG [1]

by

BELLA AND SAMUEL SPEWACK

The scene is MRS. SOLOMON'S *paper stand on a street on the lower east side of New York. It is about ten o'clock of a spring evening.* MRS. SOLOMON *is a middle-aged Jewish woman, kind and too generous for her slim purse. A woman of great strength of character, she has uncomplainingly suffered many hardships to support her two daughters.* FREIBERG, *proprietor of a neighboring butcher shop, is her staunch friend. He, too, believes in doing only what is right and good. He is "groping, charmingly inarticulate."*

FREIBERG *is still perplexed. He emerges from the stand and looks up the street. Finally* MRS. SOLOMON *comes from the house.*

MRS. SOLOMON. Where's Florrie?

FREIBERG. You left Florrie by the stand?

[1] Copyright, 1936, by Bella and Samuel Spewack.

MRS. SOLOMON. Sure. . . . Where is she?

FREIBERG. I dunno. When I come out from my store there was nobody here.   *where's Tilly?*

MRS. SOLOMON. (*Horrified.*) She left the stand alone! That girl! Couldn't sit here ten minutes. She went to Charley's—with Birdie. (*Sighs.*)

FREIBERG. It's a good thing I was here. You'd a lost a customer for matches.

MRS. SOLOMON. (*Sighs again.*) What should I do with her? Tonight all of a sudden she wants to get married before Tillie. And she begins to cry—

FREIBERG. And by tomorrow she won't want to get married.

MRS. SOLOMON. Maybe. (*Sits down on bench.*) Honest, Freiberg, she's my own child but from one minute to the next I don't know her. Do you remember by us in Europe, at night, in the summer—the little flies that light up—

FREIBERG. Fireflies—

MRS. SOLOMON. That's Florrie!—Closed your store? (FREIBERG *nods.*) I think I'll close the stand, too. (*Begins preparations for closing the stand, folding papers, etc.* FREIBERG *helps her. This is a nightly routine with them.*)

FREIBERG. I'm going to the bank tomorrow morning. You got anything to deposit?

MRS. SOLOMON. Not today. Florrie cleaned me out.

FREIBERG. I still got your bank book. (*Taking book from pocket.*) You want it?

MRS. SOLOMON. (*Taking it.*) Four hundred and eighty-nine dollars in twelve years— (*Puts it in her bosom.*)

FREIBERG. You're rich!

MRS. SOLOMON. You know, Freiberg, I couldn't help thinking when I was waiting for Segal today in his big house, how he started with us right here with a little bakery and today he's a millionaire. You know, they say he's got a hundred thousand dollars!

FREIBERG. You think he's happy?

MRS. SOLOMON. Well, his children don't have to wait to get married.

FREIBERG. So they got other troubles. You think the rich are happy? They eat more. Fancier. So they get sick. They sleep longer. Softer. Warmer on cold nights. So in the least draft they catch a cold.

MRS. SOLOMON. Tolstoy!

FREIBERG. Tolstoy said the simple life is the best life. You know he was a rich man—a prince—but he didn't feel good, so he became a shoemaker, and he felt fine.

MRS. SOLOMON. If he had a stand, he wouldn't feel so fine.

FREIBERG. The more books you read, the less you care about money.

MRS. SOLOMON. That must be the trouble with me. I can't read.

FREIBERG. You're missing a lot. There's so much to read. You should learn. A smart woman like you should read and write English. Even for your business. When a man asks for a newspaper—

MRS. SOLOMON. Tillie puts them in the places—*Journal*— *Telegram*—*News*. And then I always say: Help yourself!

FREIBERG. I'll learn you—

MRS. SOLOMON. Who's got time?

FREIBERG. After the children get married, and you sell the stand—

MRS. SOLOMON. Ach, Freiberg, it's too late.

FREIBERG. But what are you goin' to do when you're alone? Why should you keep on with the stand? I got a fine store— a little money—who am I working for? We can live out our old age together and I'll learn you English.

MRS. SOLOMON. (*She winces suddenly, strokes her legs.*) Ach . . . my feet . . . It's gonna rain. . . . (*Sits down.*)

FREIBERG. You know, I think so, too . . . I feel it in the back.

MRS. SOLOMON. (*With a wry smile.*) Freiberg, sometimes I feel sorry for my feet— (*Looking down at them.*)

FREIBERG. That's from the stand.

MRS. SOLOMON. (*Smiles.*) The simple life is the best life! (*Rubs her legs—rises again.*) Freiberg, it's late. And you gotta get up early tomorrow. Go. Good night, Freiberg.

FREIBERG. Mrs. Solomon—Jacob waited seven years for his Leah. How long must I wait for you?

MRS. SOLOMON. (*Evasively, shyly.*) Freiberg—don't forget. Put away a chicken for Mrs. Reuben. Only don't tell her you're giving it to her. She won't take it. Say it's for trust.

FREIBERG. All right—all right— (*He moves.*) You don't wanna answer me. All right— (*Trying to exit.*)

MRS. SOLOMON. Freiberg—

FREIBERG. (*Pause.*) Yes!

MRS. SOLOMON. (*Smiling wearily.*) Freiberg, when the children are married, ask me again, if you don't mind.

FREIBERG. Why not? Good night, Mrs. Solomon. (*He exits.*)

MRS. SOLOMON. Good night, Freiberg. (*She turns out the light of the stand. She begins putting up the boards.*)

THE GOOD FAIRY [1]

by

FERENC MOLNAR

Translated and adapted by Jane Hinton

LU *is a most delightful young woman. She is unique and her air of naïveté is very disarming. She is willing to sacrifice her own well-being to achieve her earnest desire to do somebody—anybody—a good deed. The scene is a private dining room in a smart hotel.* LU *is waiting for her host who has gone to call for another member of the party. The* WAITER *is a nondescript sort of person. He is in love with* LU.

WAITER. Why all the elegant talk?

LU. I'm not talking. I'm making conversation. Please don't give me away! I told him I was a lady . . . a society lady! . . .

[1] Copyright, 1932, by Charles Frohman, Inc. Reprinted by permission of the Crown Publishers.

WAITER. The dress?

LU. Borrowed. (*Weeps.*)

WAITER. Why are you crying?

LU. Please don't give me away!

WAITER. Oh! What do you think I am? . . .

LU. If he knew that I'm only a movie usherette . . . A sort of glow worm . . . with my flashlight blinking in the dark . . . all dressed in lemon yellow coat and glaring red skirt. . . .

WAITER. (*Crossing to center table.*) You watch out that some day he doesn't wander into the movie theater.

LU. Oh, I left the movie theater a week ago. For his sake. He respects me so. . . .

WAITER. Then—what do you live on?

LU. Oh, I eat a lot of cakes at the dansants! And then, I've saved a little . . . enough for two weeks . . . And I have debts, too! . . . Nice, big ones!

WAITER. Debts! Who would give you credit? (*Sits at table.*)

LU. Everybody! Everybody likes me! (*Sadly.*) That's why I have so many debts! (*She drinks.*) Board bills, dressmakers, shoemakers, hairdressers, manicures, sleepingpowders, permanent waves, reducing tablets, dentists, cigarettes, eau de Cologne, powder, rouge, magazines, dog license . . . all on credit! There's only one person to whom I pay cash. . . .

WAITER. Who?

LU. The beggar. (*Drinks.*) That's because I expect that some day he'll have to support me. . . . I don't know what I am. What do you think? . . . Am I a working girl? (WAITER *tries to speak.*) No . . . and yet, that would be my ideal! But, I can't work.

WAITER. Too bad. . . .

LU. I can't work. . . . (*Pause.*) Do you know what I'd like to be?

WAITER. What?

LU. An idiot. They say idiots are happy.

WAITER. Do you think you're so wise?

LU. No. But I'm not an idiot, either! Fifty-fifty. And that's the worst of all! But—God loves me. . . . Because I'm good. Am I not?

WAITER. Oh, yes.

LU. I do good whenever I can. Do you know what I am?

WAITER. What?

LU. A fairy! (*She drinks.*) I have no one. Have I?

WAITER. If you say so. And if you don't count me. (LU *pulls something out of the corner of her chair.*)

LU. What is this?

WAITER. Good Lord! Baron Hell's gold cigarette case! We've been hunting for it all week. I've even been to the police about it! Where was it?

LU. Right here. It had slipped down in the corner.

WAITER. You darling! You can't imagine how happy you've made me! They even suspected me!

LU. (*Looks at* WAITER *and goes to table.*) Now, you see? I found it without even looking for it!

WAITER. You really *are* a fairy!

LU. Oh, I am!

PRESENTING HISTORICAL AND PERIOD SCENES

PARNELL [1]

by

ELSIE T. SCHAUFFLER

CHARLES PARNELL *is the leader of the Irish Party. "He is tall, dark-haired, slender, a man between 30, and 35. Very pale, curiously burning dark eyes. His manner, unconsciously aloof is very quiet. The relation between himself and his Party workers is almost that of a schoolmaster, adored yet feared by his pupils." He has worked for years on the issue of Irish Home Rule. Just when this work is about to be realized, a personal indiscretion is made into a political issue by his enemies. The Party is split and it has come to a question of whether PARNELL is to be supported any longer.*

PARNELL. Good evening, gentlemen. . . . This is in no sense a formal meeting but a gathering of leaders to talk over our future policy. . . . In regard to the steps we must take to insure a safe majority for the Home Rule Bill. . . . Sixteen years ago I conceived the idea of an Irish Party welded into one complete whole. All the different factions of Ireland fighting together for one purpose, the freedom of Ireland. Our Party oath "Sit together, act together, vote together." (*Cries of "aye," "That we have," etc.*) I knew that only by presenting a common front to the enemy could we hope for victory. Ten years ago I was elected leader of that Party. (*There is dead silence.*) You have given me absolute loyalty, absolute obedience, and we have at last forced on the English

[1] Copyright, 1934, by Elsie T. Schauffler; copyright, 1936, by Samuel French.

the necessity of granting Home Rule to Ireland. *("Hear." "Hear.")* By our votes the Liberals have been swept to power. In return Mr. Gladstone promised us Home Rule. He was to move the first reading of the Bill this session. Now, for personal reasons, which I shall not discuss here— . . . Mr. Gladstone refuses to continue his support because he objects to me, personally, as Leader of the Irish Party. . . . *(He rises slowly to his feet. He has that queer calmness of manner, that strange aloofness which made him so irresistible to the Irish people.)* In a public letter Mr. Gladstone demands my resignation. Putting aside the question of what right he, or any other Englishman, has to dictate to us, I say, putting this aside, although I consider it fundamental, I have replied to Mr. Gladstone. Since I am no longer acceptable to him as Leader of the Irish Party, I have told him I will resign at once. *(There is a complete hush over the room.)* —If he will give me his assurance— . . . *(As though there had been no interruption.)* I said I would resign if he would give me his word that he would continue to support the Home Rule Bill. Gentlemen, Mr. Healy and Mr. Redmond have just left Mr. Gladstone. I have not talked to them. Mr. Healy, will you tell us the result of your visit. . . . Did he, or did he not promise to support Home Rule? . . . *(He did not.)* If you think you can fight Gladstone without me, that is for you to decide, but—don't sell me for nothing. If you surrender me—if you throw me to him—it is your bounden duty to secure value for the sacrifice. *(He pauses and looks at them.)* I have a Parliament in the hollow of my hand. I give you my word I will get it for you— if you will let me.

ABRAHAM LINCOLN [1]

by

JOHN DRINKWATER

In the following scene we see ABRAHAM LINCOLN *at the age of 50, in his home at Springfield, Illinois, in the year 1860. The tall, gaunt figure is slightly stooped. The sensitiveness to others, the simplicity and the fortitude that have come to be associated with the man, are apparent. A delegation has been sent inviting* LINCOLN *to become Republican candidate for the office of President. Before accepting he asks them:*

LINCOLN. Gentlemen, I am known to one of you only. Do you know my many disqualifications for this work? . . . There are some, shall we say graces, that I lack. Washington does not altogether neglect these. . . . Do not be under any misunderstanding, I beg you. I aim at moderation so far as it is honest. But I am a very stubborn man, gentlemen. If the South insists upon the extension of slavery, and claims the right to secede, as you know it very well may do, and the decision lies with me, it will mean resistance, inexorable, with blood if needs be. I would have everybody's mind clear as to that. . . . If you send me, the South will have little but derision for your choice. . . . I can take any man's ridicule— I'm trained to it by a . . . somewhat odd figure that it pleased God to give me, if I may so far be pleasant with you. But this slavery business will be long and deep, and bitter. I know it. If you do me this honor, gentlemen, you must look to me for no compromise in this matter. If abolition comes in due time by constitutional means, good. I want it. But, while we will not force abolition, we will give slavery no approval, and we will not allow it to extend its boundaries by one yard. The determination is in my blood. When I was a boy I made a trip to New Orleans, and there I saw them, chained, beaten, kicked as a man would be ashamed to kick a thieving dog. And I saw a young girl driven up and down the room that the bidders might satisfy themselves. And I said then, "If ever I get a chance to hit that thing, I'll hit it hard." (*A pause.*) You have no conditions to make? . . . I wouldn't have you think it graceless of me to be slow in my answer. But once given, it's for the deep good or the deep ill of all this country. In the face of that a man may well ask himself twenty times, when he's twenty times sure. You make no qualification, any one among you? . . . I thank you. I accept.

JAYHAWKER [1]

by

SINCLAIR LEWIS AND LLOYD LEWIS

ACE BURDETTE *started his career as a lawyer. Soon he became one of the leaders of the Jayhawkers, a group of men who drove slavery out of Kansas before the beginning of the Civil War. A loquacious speaker, he stumped his way across Kansas wheedling and lying his way into the United States Senate to fight slavery. After three years of war, he is shocked by it. He is talking with an old friend, a southern general, who was captured by the Yankees. He is being sent home in trade for a northern officer.*

ACE. Smallwood, I guess, of all the fire-eaters, you was the fire-eatin'est. . . . It seemed differ'nt then. Tell me, Smallwood, did you have any idee what war was like—a *real* war? . . . This is the third time we've invaded Virginny. Right soon, America's going to be so weak our European

[1] Copyright, 1935, by Sinclair Lewis and Lloyd Lewis.

friends will step in here and take charge—and then, . . .
you'll see a Hapsburg king in Washington! When the
French put the Emperor Maximilian in Mexico—Whee!—
they knocked the Monroe Doctrine to smithereens! Somebody ought to stop us Americans killin' each other. . . .
Them as started it should stop it, shouldn't they? . . . You
know how fierce I've been to crush this rebellion. I've de-
manded yer leaders be hanged as traitors, and yer niggers
be freed and given yer land and made voters. And there's a
lot of Senators with me for vengeance. If they ever got wind
of what I kinda got a sudden idee I'm now goin' to propose
to you, they'd set up such a holler that before I could launch
my craft they'd nip it in the bud. Our only chance is to
trick 'em—spring it on 'em quick. . . . Here's my idee:
All at once Grant and Lee announce a truce. An hour later,
your President and *our* President issue a call for both sides
to join hands agin the French in Mexico. You rebs come
back into the Union, with your slaves freed but not votin'—
not for a generation, anyway. You keep your other property
and get all your old rights back. The two armies march off
side by side under *General Jeff Davis!*—march clear to
Texas and on into Mexico—annex it, of course—and then
maybe right on into South America. . . . We statesmen on
each side'll whoop it for a war against the furriners. But
it'd all have to be a complete surprise—understand?

VICTORIA REGINA [1]

by

Laurence Housman

It is the year 1859. VICTORIA *has been queen of England
about 22 years. She has learned, by this time, to consult*
PRINCE ALBERT *on all her questions of state. He is invaluable*

to her, and she is devoted to him. Never under any cir-
cumstances does she forget her position. She is addressing
DR. STANLEY.

THE QUEEN. Oh, good morning, Dr. Stanley. How very good
of you to come, and so punctually! I wanted you to be here
this morning. . . . Do, please, sit down. . . . You see, Dr.
Stanley, I and the Prince have always felt that we ought—
as far as we could—to encourage our distinguished men of
literature. But there is always this difficulty. It is quite impossible to have at my Court, in the ordinary way, those with
whom I cannot take the lead . . . intellectually, I mean, in
conversation. I can, of course, make certain exceptions. Mr.
Tennyson comes to me sometimes; and though I have not
read many of his poems myself, he reads them to me; so
conversation becomes unnecessary. . . . Oh, yes; (I enjoy
the readings) for even without understanding the poems,
one can praise his reading of them. He has a beautiful voice;
and he is so picturesque—so like a poet, is he not? . . .
Besides, he really is, I suppose, a great poet. . . . There was
just a question of offering the post (of Laureate) to Lord
Macaulay, whose *Lays of Ancient Rome* are certainly the
finest poetry I know. But it was thought that would perhaps
be too political an appointment. Mr. Tennyson, I understand, has no politics. . . . Well, that was really settled for
us by the Prime Minister. But often since, in other cases, it
has been a great regret that one could not pay all the attention one would like—by commanding their attendance at
Court—to those who, outside politics, have become eminent
in literature. . . . Of course some of the Bishops have written books, I know. But it is as Bishops, not authors that they
come here. And of course, being Head of the Church, I feel
myself their equal, though we don't talk theology . . . Nor
have we any difficulty about artists. Their minds are not
remarkable in thought or conversation; they are quite quiet
and modest, I mean—waiting until they are spoken to. Sir
Edwin Landseer, for instance, is a great artist, one of the

greatest of all ages; but when he talks, he is just like anyone else—quite modest and pleasant. And he does not mind his work being criticised; though I believe, he knows more about dogs than I do. . . . Books are different. If I am to meet an author, I feel I must have read one of his books, at least, and been able to understand it. And as I really have not time for doing so, that is one of the reasons why I cannot—except on very special occasions—have authors coming to my Court.

PARNELL [1]

by

ELSIE T. SCHAUFFLER

The scene is the PRIME MINISTER'S *study at 10 Downing Street. It is late in an afternoon in November about 1890.* MR. GLADSTONE *is at his desk. He is past middle-age—a big man and heavy set.* TIMOTHY HEALY *is one of* PARNELL'S *young associates. Pleasant, serious, he is neither shrewd enough nor experienced enough to match wits with* GLADSTONE. *Nor is he strong enough to withstand* GLADSTONE'S *subtle flattery.*

GLADSTONE. (*Rises from his chair with hand outstretched. He is beaming genially though perhaps, for the sensitive, a shade too patronizing. The smiling blue eyes can turn to slate, and the smiling mouth to a hard, straight line.*) My dear Mr. Healy, (HEALY *crosses to* GLADSTONE *who shakes hands with him.*) how very good of you to come.

HEALY. (*Bowing awkwardly. Unfamiliar with this kind of thing.*) Prime Minister.

GLADSTONE. Will you smoke?

HEALY. Thank you, no, Sir.

GLADSTONE. Do sit down, Mr. Healy. (HEALY *sits.*) One can so often arrive (GLADSTONE *sits.*) at the solution of a problem if one can talk face to face.

HEALY. I can scarcely hope for such an outcome in the present instance, Sir.

GLADSTONE. Why not, Mr. Healy?

HEALY. Mr. Gladstone, you promised the Irish Party that you would bring in the Home Rule Bill. You have not done so. I do not see much room for argument in the matter.

GLADSTONE. Whatever I may have promised, I promised to Mr. Parnell.

HEALY. He *is* the Irish Party, Mr. Gladstone.

GLADSTONE. There, I am sorry, I cannot agree with you. How is he? I heard he had been ill.

HEALY. Very ill. He has recovered, however.

GLADSTONE. I cannot tell you how much he has been in my thoughts. Poor fellow, poor fellow. . . . Ah—a dominant personality—an unbending will. (*Comes forward.*) You will pardon me if I say that I have sometimes wondered how a man of your keen mind, and strength of character, could at all times submit yourself to the complete dominance of even a Parnell.

HEALY. I am proud to serve under him.

GLADSTONE. Ah—you are very modest, Mr. Healy, exceedingly modest. Parnell *is* wonderful of course. What a tragedy! Poor fellow, what a fall!

HEALY. I was not aware of any fall, Sir. Parnell is still Leader of the Irish Party.

GLADSTONE. His continued leadership, Mr. Healy, would be fatal to the Irish cause.

HEALY. I do not agree with you, Sir.

GLADSTONE. His usefulness is at an end. . . . Do not think me antagonistic—unsympathetic—

HEALY. I cannot reconcile your sympathetic thoughts with your actions, Mr. Gladstone. You have issued a public letter, printed in the newspapers, in which you say that unless Parnell resigns you will feel called upon to do so.

GLADSTONE. (*Smiling quietly.*) Did I say I would resign, Mr. Healy?

HEALY. You said—well—everyone took it to mean that. What did you mean, Mr. Gladstone?

GLADSTONE. I think I cannot usefully add to what I have already written. . . .

HEALY. Because he has gone wrong in a private question is that a reason why he should fail in his duty to his people?

GLADSTONE. (*In a ringing voice.*) He would not fail. Others will fail him.

HEALY. (*Fighting back.*) We shall not. I'm sure of that.

GLADSTONE. (*Strong. Deadly definite. His eyes piercing steel.*) Are you—Mr. Healy—*Sure?* The leader of the Irish Party is enveloped in the nauseous fumes of the divorce court. They rise to Heaven, and yet you persist in a policy which bids fair to wreck your Party. Is Mr. Parnell the only Irishman capable of leading you? Are the forceful, brilliant men of your Party a lot of weaklings? No, Mr. Healy, I am impressed with your modesty but I find it deplorable.

HEALY. (*Less certainly, more pleadingly.*) He has led us forth out of the wilderness. We are within sight of the Promised Land—

GLADSTONE. Call upon your knowledge of Scripture further, Mr. Healy. Remember, Moses was allowed to see but not to enter the Promised Land. God knows how I regret being the instrument chosen for the downfall of such a man. But I cannot be entirely wrong in my estimate of the mettle of the Irish Party. I cannot but feel that the Irish cause is greater than the fall of one man. Do you not agree with me, Mr. Healy?

HEALY. I do not know, Mr. Gladstone.

GLADSTONE. Ah—you wish only to do what is wisest and best. There is a hope in my heart that there shall arise some day a new and greater leader. One with whom I could join hands. Ah, what could we not do for Ireland. I shall pray to that end. (*Planted—firm—brusque. Holding out his hand*.) You were good to come to me, Mr. Healy. I thank you.

HEALY. I am most sensible of the honor and most grateful. Good afternoon. (*He bows and goes out through the ante-room*.)

BRITTLE HEAVEN [1]

by

VINCENT YORK AND FREDERICK POHL

EMILY DICKINSON *lives in Amherst, Mass. She is a very shy person, charming and sensitive. Her friend,* HELEN, *although clever and witty, is also frivolous and conceited. She misunderstood her husband's admiration for* EMILY *and her poetry. Using her political influence she has* MAJOR HUNT *transferred from his scientific work to active service in the Civil War. This only forces the issue and* EMILY *and* MAJOR HUNT *declare their love for each other. Reminded of her childhood pledge of eternal friendship to* HELEN, EMILY *sends the* MAJOR *away. Two years pass.* EMILY *grows pale. She sees none of her friends and is unable to write.* HELEN *comes to Amherst to see her.*

HELEN. (*Enters right, animated as usual*.) Emily! I'm so glad to *see* you!

EMILY. (*Taking* HELEN's *hand but making no move to kiss her*.) We meet again, Helen.

HELEN. (*Troubled*.) You don't look well.

EMILY. It's nothing.

HELEN. (*Truly concerned*.) But, Emily, you— (*Breaks off embarrassed*.)

EMILY. Do sit down; tell me all about yourself. (*There is a moment of constraint as* HELEN *sits left end of sofa;* EMILY *chair left center.*) You've been writing!

HELEN. (*Brightening.*) You saw my verse in the *Atlantic.* . . . Mr. Higginson encouraged. He's been adorable. Heaven knows, I need moral support.

EMILY. You, with the world at your feet.

HELEN. (*Biting her lip.*) Scarcely that but at least I have the courage to make a new start.

EMILY. Helen?—nothing has—*happened?*

HELEN. A great deal has happened.

EMILY. (*Her apprehension growing.*) Nothing to—Edward?

HELEN. (*Emotionally.*) Of course something has happened to Edward.

EMILY. (*Rising.*) Not—

HELEN. Oh, he's *safe;* don't worry. Or was, the last I knew.

EMILY. (*Taking a step center.*) Then what do you mean?

HELEN. Emily, don't make it hard for me.

EMILY. (*With tears in her eyes.*) Truly, I never meant—

HELEN. For weeks I shut myself in my room. The world was ashes in my heart.

EMILY. (*Astounded.*) When was this!

HELEN. Two years ago, after that awful day—at summer's full.

EMILY. I should have thought it a day of rejoicing for you.

HELEN. Because my rival won?

EMILY. Won?

HELEN. Whatever you may think about me, I loved him too. (*Throwing off her mood.*) But it's all over now. I have a new philosophy of life. That's why I came to Amherst. I felt able at last to confess the truth.

EMILY. What truth?

HELEN. You thought you gave Edward back to me.

EMILY. (*Tremulous—turning somewhat away from* HELEN.) As if there were any doubt!

HELEN. You thought in your innocence words could perform miracles.

EMILY. (*Beside herself.*) I gave him back. . . .

HELEN. (*Gently.*) He has continued to love you, to this day!

EMILY. (*Thunderstruck; staring at* HELEN.) He—what?

HELEN. I said he has continued to love you, Emily.

EMILY. After I failed him!

HELEN. Your failure was your strength! (*As* EMILY *turns away.*) Oh, yes, I know; you were to meet him. I also know that instead of going, you wrote, "Nowhere on Earth!" . . . You won him most by keeping our pledge of friendship. . . . (*With chin high.*) But I have come to show that I can keep a pledge of friendship too. I came to tell you, that much as you wished to, you could not give him back. He will remain yours to his dying day.

EMILY. (*With eyes afar.*) Mine! . . . Where is he stationed?

HELEN. (*Biting her lip—gives way right to sofa.*) I don't know where he is.

EMILY. (*Aghast as the idea penetrates her mind.*) His own *wife* not know—

HELEN. (*Sitting sofa.*) I've been up *North* most of the summer.

EMILY. (*Following her.*) But there have been letters?

HELEN. Not since July. (*As* EMILY *looks more aghast than ever.*) And that one posted a month earlier in Virginia.

EMILY. (*Vigorously.*) Then he's still there with his artillery regiment.

HELEN. (*Shaking her head.*) He was mysteriously transferred to the War Office. I was in Boston at the time; before I could reach Washington he had been sent away.

EMILY. Where?

HELEN. (*Significantly.*) They wouldn't tell me. . . . There were hints about New York.

EMILY. (*Turning.*) New York? Then he's back in the Coast Survey again!

HELEN. Or the secret service.

EMILY. (*Accusingly.*) You have no idea at all where he is?

HELEN. None, Emily. Please be sensible. Oh, it just seemed as tho I couldn't go on any longer without telling you the truth.

EMILY. (*Closing in—angry.*) You've done it to punish me.

HELEN. Emily Dickinson!

EMILY. (*At left end of sofa.*) When I was already insane with dread!

HELEN. (*Shrinking.*) I did no such thing; I swear!

EMILY. Just for revenge!

HELEN. (*In tears.*) It's ungenerous of you.

EMILY. (*More and more inquisitorial.*) Giving me false hopes, just for the satisfaction of seeing me sink into worse despair!

HELEN. (*Frantic.*) I came solely to prove that I was your friend.

EMILY. Friends can be pain.

HELEN. Emily, you *can't* be like this again. It's cruel of you.

EMILY. I don't trust you. (*Savagely.*) I believe you know where to find him.

HELEN. After all I've suffered! That doesn't sound like my Emily.

EMILY. Helen!—you *do know!*

HELEN. I don't! I don't!

EMILY. Is that the truth?

HELEN. It's the truth, God help me!

EMILY. (*With hands clasped as in prayer.*) God help us *both!* (*Dropping on her knees, head in* HELEN's *lap.*) God help us both!

LADY PRECIOUS STREAM [1]

An old Chinese play adapted by

S. I. HSIUNG

LADY PRECIOUS STREAM *is the youngest and most charming daughter of the* PRIME MINISTER *of China. Against her fa-*

[NOTE: In the Chinese theatre there is no attempt at realism. The property man is on the stage almost constantly, moving the props as the lines indicate, and assisting the actors as he sees fit. Nor do the Chinese use scenery. The dressing of the stage is left entirely to the imagination of the audience.]

ther's wishes she marries HSIEH PING-KUEI, *gardener and poet. Despite their poverty they are very happy in the cave that is their home. Because of bravery* HSIEH *is appointed a captain in the Western Punitive Expedition. Nearly a year passes and* HSIEH *is reported dead.* PRECIOUS STREAM *is ill from worry and her brother-in-law refuses to send her the rice and firewood which is the captain's pay.* MADAM, *her mother, comes to visit. She is a sweet-faced, soft-spoken woman.*

PRECIOUS STREAM. Dear mother, allow me to kneel down and pay my respects to you.

MADAM. (*Stopping her.*) No, you mustn't stand on ceremony.

PRECIOUS STREAM. (*Kneeling down and kotowing.*) Your unfilial daughter has neglected you too long to be pardoned! Let her redeem her sin by kneeling before you to beg forgiveness!

MADAM. (*Taking her into her arms again.*) Don't, my darling. It is your forgiveness that we should all beg. . . . I have heard that you are hungry and cold, and you are not well. So I wanted to see you and the place where you are living.

PRECIOUS STREAM. (*Barring the way.*) Oh, no! My humble cave would profane your dignity.

MADAM. Nonsense! I must go in and see what kind of a life you are leading.

PRECIOUS STREAM. It is a small, wretched hole and would only make you feel uncomfortable.

MADAM. (*Firmly.*) The place where my dear daughter can live for nearly a year is at least good enough for me to visit!

PRECIOUS STREAM. (*Giving in.*) Then let me go in first and have the place tidied for you.

MADAM. No, I want to see it just as it is. Lead the way, my darling. (*They turn and enter the cave.*)

PRECIOUS STREAM. Mind the steps, dear mother!

MADAM. (*Looking around.*) So this is your place! Oh, you

silly darling, fancy your forsaking your beautifully decorated boudoir and coming to this horrible cave! How could you?

PRECIOUS STREAM. (*Offering her a broken chair.*) Make yourself comfortable in this poor chair, dear mother. I am afraid I have no tea or refreshments to offer you, except some poor rice. (*She takes a small bowl and a pair of chopsticks and presents them to* MADAM.)

MADAM. (*Receiving them and putting them down after a glance at them.*) Fancy your sacrificing the delicacies you enjoyed for this poor stuff! How could you? Now, sit down yourself.

PRECIOUS STREAM. (*Sitting on left side.*) Thank you, dear mother! After those delicacies this plain fare seemed to be very palatable to me.

MADAM. You are under-nourished. That's why you are ill.

PRECIOUS STREAM. Indeed it is not a question of food. The wretch Wei told me that my husband had been killed! It was this news that sent me to bed.

MADAM. This news may be false, darling.

PRECIOUS STREAM. Oh, yes! I don't believe it at all. But, still, it makes me feel wretched. And father sends agents to try to persuade me to marry again, which makes me feel worse.

MADAM. (*Furious.*) The old rascal! He'll wish he'd never been born when I've done talking to him tonight!

PRECIOUS STREAM. Oh, no! Please don't quarrel with my father on *my* account. It will only increase my sin against filial piety.

MADAM. Very well then. He has you to thank if I let him off. How are you feeling now?

PRECIOUS STREAM. You see I have already recovered at the sight of you!

MADAM. But this is not the place for convalescence. Now be reasonable, and come back with your mother to our house, where you need not worry about anything, and will have plenty to eat and plenty to wear.

PRECIOUS STREAM. No, dear mother. I made a solemn wager with father, confirming it by clapping our hands together three times, that I would never return to the Prime Minister's house until we are quite rich and prosperous.

MADAM. But you will be starved if you stay here.

PRECIOUS STREAM. I'd rather starve here than go back.

MADAM. Foolish child!

PRECIOUS STREAM. I am too proud to lower my flag of independence. . . .

MADAM. But since you refuse to go with me, I will stay with you here instead.

PRECIOUS STREAM. (*Frightened.*) Oh, no! This is not a place for you to stay.

MADAM. I am determined. The place where my darling may live is at least good enough for me to stay a few nights.

PRECIOUS STREAM. (*Troubled, pacing the stage.*) This will never do! This will never do! (*Aside to herself.*) What shall I do? (*She taps her forehead with her fingers.*) Ah, I have it! (*To* MADAM.) Well, mother, I have changed my mind. I agree to return with you rather than to let you stay here with me.

MADAM. (*Pleased.*) That's a good girl! . . . Then come at once! (*She gets up and starts.*)

PRECIOUS STREAM. (*Assisting her Mother.*) Mind the steps, mother. . . . Oh, mother, I forgot something. . . . I forgot to lock the cave door.

MADAM. Never mind. I will tell the maid to lock it for you.

PRECIOUS STREAM. And I forgot to put the silver, the rice, and the clothes in a safe place.

MADAM. They won't be lost if the cave door is locked.

PRECIOUS STREAM. But the rats. They will eat the rice and destroy the clothes. (*This is undoubtedly quite true.*) . . . I can't allow anything from my dear mother to be destroyed. I won't be a moment. . . . (*Running into the cave and closing the door quickly.*) Mother, I am not going back with you! And for my unfilial conduct I am kneeling inside the cave. (*She kneels and weeps aloud.*)

MADAM. (*Realizing her daughter's plan.*) Oh, my obstinate darling! How could you? (*She weeps too.*)

PRECIOUS STREAM. (*Amidst her sobs.*) Dear mother, though I remain in the cave, my heart goes with you!

MADAM. (*Weeping.*) Oh, my poor darling daughter!

PRECIOUS STREAM. (*Weeping.*) Oh, my poor dear mother! (*The small procession starts again, with* MADAM *crying in the carriage, and proceeds on its way.*)

PRECIOUS STREAM. (*Crying all the time.*) Oh, she has gone! (*She gets up and retires.*)

PRIDE AND PREJUDICE [1]

by

HELEN JEROME

From Jane Austen's novel

The BENNETTS *live in Loungbourn, England, in 1796.* ELIZABETH, *the eldest, is quite a modern young woman for her time. She is intelligent, charming and rather outspoken.* MR. COLLINS, *her cousin, is a clergyman. He is a combination of piety, self-importance and servility. Visiting Loungbourn for a few weeks for the express purpose of choosing a wife, he thus confers the honor.*

ELIZABETH *enters from door up left.*

ELIZABETH. Oh, Mr. Collins, have you finished your sermon? (*As she notes his idiotic fatuous smirk . . . she fears the worst and makes for the door up right, to escape.*) If you'll excuse me (*As Collins puts out a detaining hand.*) . . . I want to go and reply to this letter from Mr. Wickham. . . .

COLLINS. (*Fondly.*) It's perfectly understandable and indeed proper that a young girl should display this modesty. . . . (*Approaches the horrified* ELIZABETH *and offers her a chair.*) Indeed, Miss Elizabeth, it is an added incentive. (*Plants himself in front of her. She sits with a sigh of resignation, her*

[1] Copyright, 1935, by Doubleday, Doran and Company, Inc.

hands in her lap, looking up at him from under her lids with a comical expression in which boredom and a secret amusement are mingled. He mistakes her silence for shyness.) You can hardly be in doubt as to what I am about to propose, my dear and lovely Elizabeth! (*Shakes head benevolently.*) Your natural delicacy may lead you to dissemble . . . but I flatter myself my attentions have been too marked to be mistaken. (*He grows more pompous every minute, and more lyrical, as he enumerates the joys he is about to bestow on her. Now he clears his throat as though about to address his congregation.*) I have singled you out as the companion of my future life. . . . (*Waits for her exclamation of wondering gratitude . . . but she is silent.*) And before my feelings run away with me . . . I owe it to you to tell you the reasons. (*The notion of his feelings running amok almost upsets her gravity, but she manages to keep her face straight. Swallowing for a fresh outburst.*) That very noble lady, my patroness, has condescended to advise me to marry and even goes so far . . . (*In a hushed voice.*) as to promise to visit . . . actually visit . . . the lady I bring to the parsonage as my wife. . . . If . . . (*Pausing solemnly.*) I choose *wisely!* (*Paces a bit then stops in front of her.*) Another reason, my fair cousin, is that I am to inherit your father's estate. It is only fitting that I keep it as far as possible in the family. (*He nows holds out his hand with a royal gesture of bestowal, quite expecting it will be instantly and gratefully accepted. It is not.*) These, dear Miss Elizabeth, are my motives and now nothing remains but to assure you of the violence of my affection. (*She is still motionless. He glances at her encouragingly, coming closer.*) I know that one thousand pounds in the four per cents is all you will have as dowry . . . and . . . (*A little ruefully.*) even *that* you will not receive until your mother's death . . . (*Pauses, then reassures her, delicately.*) but you can rest assured that on *that* score no ungenerous reproach shall ever pass my lips after we are married.

ELIZABETH. (*Slowly.*) Aren't you a little hasty, sir? (*Pause, as he takes her hand and encouragingly pats it. She withdraws it politely.*) You seem to forget that I have made no answer to this dazzling offer! (*He smiles at her fondly, enchanted with her maidenly pretense of refusal.*) I appreciate the honor you seem to feel you have done me . . . (*He falls on one knee, raises her hand which he had to grab for, to his lips. She moves back so quickly that she nearly upsets him.*) and I decline it with thanks. (*She rises as though to end the interview. He regains his feet, smiles fondly, gazing at her with his head on one side.*)

COLLINS. Indeed, I understand, dear Miss Elizabeth . . . yes, it is quite a charming and delicate custom for young ladies to say *No,* when they mean *Yes.* (*Archly, shaking a finger at her.*) I am therefore not at all discouraged and shall hope to lead you to the altar before very long.

ELIZABETH. (*Astonished and getting exasperated.*) Upon my word, sir, you are difficult to discourage. (*He shakes his head, smiling fatuously.*) I assure you I am *not* one of those idiotic young ladies you describe, if indeed they exist outside of novels. Difficult as it seems for you to believe it . . . I will *not* marry you. You could not make *me* happy, and I certainly could not make *you* . . . (*Moves further away.*) and I have no ambition at all to try. (*He smiles with amused fondness.*) And if your friend the Lady Catherine de Bourgh really knew me, she would utterly disapprove of me for the exalted position you offer.

COLLINS. (*Suddenly sobered.*) Oh! . . . if I thought Lady Catherine would disapprove! (*Reflects, looks her up and down.*) Ah, but *no* . . . impossible! You can be sure that when I have the honor of seeing her ladyship again I shall speak in the highest terms of your modesty and economy. (*Nods several times at her, reassuringly.*)

ELIZABETH. (*By this time is so incensed that she opens and closes her mouth, lost for words. Getting nearer exit, by degrees, door up left.*) Mr. Collins, you will seriously annoy me if you say another word on this subject. . . . Go home to your patroness and ask *her* to choose for you. . . . Better select a young woman with a humbler and more contrite heart. . . . (*Smiles.*) Such a peculiar combination of conceit and humility as yours . . . will need her.

COLLINS. (*Following her and using a voice full of gentleness and what he fondly imagines is persuasion.*) When I renew my offer, I know I shall receive a more favorable answer. Believe me, dear Miss Elizabeth, I admire your modesty . . . and perfectly understand it . . . only it isn't kind to call me conceited. Humble—yes—I trust that even realizing the advantages I am offering you, I am maintaining a humble heart.

ELIZABETH. (*Contemplating him with astonishment.*) If what I have said sounds like encouragement, I should be interested to know what you would regard as a refusal?

COLLINS. I am too well aware, dear Cousin, that it is by no means certain that any other gentleman will ever make you an offer, (*Smiles forgivingly.*) so I naturally understand that your rejection of my suit is according to the usual practice of elegant females.

ELIZABETH. (*Almost bursting into laughter.*) I see! Well, if you can, you'd better stop thinking of me as an elegant female. Just picture me as a *rational* creature, with a most inelegant habit of speaking the truth.

COLLINS. (*Seizing her hand and kissing it.*) Ah, you are quite adorable! I am certain now that when my proposal is formally sanctioned by your excellent parents, you will plainly say yes. (*She gives him one look of fury and dashes out through door up left. He pirouettes a little, fixing his collar, bobbing his head, showing the various signs of satisfaction of the self-considered lady-killer.*)

BUILDING A SCENE TO A CLIMAX

BRUTE FORCE [1]

by

JACINTO BENAVENTE

English version by John Garrett Underhill

FRED, *a circus acrobat, fell and permanently injured himself. His troupe are leaving the city and have been to the hospital to say good-bye. He is in love with one of the performers. Now that he is disabled, he is afraid she will not marry him. He is talking to a nurse.*

FRED. You see, my—my whole life is marching away. What is left? They are going to the ring, to my life and my joy, and I am staying behind, forever. The smiles are hushed for me, the companionship, the laughter, the feats in the air, the rivalries of the big nights, the shouts and the applause that lift us upon wings of light, that outprice the whole of this dull life till gladly we would catapult ourselves from the peak of the tent to the sawdust of the ring in one last magnificent arc if only we could know that a whirlwind of applause, not the shrill shriek of fear, would greet our ears as we dashed in bloody fragments on the hallowed circus ground! . . . What am I now? Look at me! A cripple, hobbling—this! This is my body that flashed like an arrow through the air, these are my legs, supple as steel, my arms, strong and enduring as iron, yet feather-light, the wings of the bird! I am broken now, set aside in the corner, a discarded toy, and my youth, my light young years are buried deep within me. I am a ruin, naked. The mason sees the

[1] Copyright, 1935, by John Garrett Underhill; copyright, 1935, by Samuel French.

house crumble upon his head and lies amid the débris entombed till he is dead. My body has crumbled and it has crushed my heart, my heart!

SEARCHING FOR THE SUN [1]

by

Dan Totheroh

DOT *is a young girl from the middle west who is forced, through the depression, to take to the road to find a job. She travels with a group of hoboes, and has fallen in love with one of them. She is a sweet girl and a plucky one. The kids are living in a Jungle camp, and they are in desperate circumstances.* DOT *is talking with* FLETCH, *one of the older members of the gang.*

DOT. How'd you know we were here? . . . Oh, you—you didn't see Matt? . . . Last night . . . he went out. . . . I . . . I thought he'd be back, early this morning . . . but . . . but he hasn't showed up yet. . . . Oh, he'll be back. . . . I . . . I jest thought . . . maybe you saw him, that's all. . . . (*Another tense pause; then* DOT *swings about.*) Fletch . . . Matt's out with Purdy! . . . (*Releasing herself . . . all in one breathless rush.*) They got big idears. . . . They think they got power now. (*Suddenly and desperately clutching* FLETCH'S *arm.*) Have people been talkin' about us, Fletch? I mean—what are they sayin' about us, along the road? . . . Do the bulls know . . . about the gun? . . . (DOT'S *head drops to her knees—as she breaks under strain. She kneels on the ground.*) You see . . . well . . . that night . . . Purdy got a gun. . . . Yes . . . Purdy got a gun . . . then Matt took it . . . an' ever since . . . Listen, Fletch . . . Matt ain't really bad. No, he ain't! He's jest mixed up . . . like all of us . . . mad at the world . . . mad

1 Copyright, 1935, by Daniel W. Totheroh (under the title *Odyssey*).

an' wantin' things. . . . Oh . . . they haven't . . . haven't
killed nobody, Fletch, if you're thinkin' that. . . . No, they
haven't. . . . I'm sure. Don't you think *I* could tell if Matt
ever did a thing like that? Jest one look . . . I could see.
. . . I could! Jest by lookin' at him, I could. He's like a little
boy, sometimes. . . . Yes, I *could* tell! You see . . . I love
him, Fletch! I love him . . . so hard . . . it hurts . . .
(*Pressing her breast*) . . . hurts all the time . . . here, I
don't know *why* I do. I can't tell you why or how it began
to be. . . . There it was . . . that pain . . . an' that sweetness . . . all of a sudden. . . . That sweetness . . . hurtin'
me. You see . . . *He* don't love me. . . . I . . . I guess I've
gone crazy, Fletch . . . an' that pride . . . all that pride I
had . . . I lost it. I had a chance at a job . . . about two
weeks ago . . . an' I wouldn't take it. You know *why* I
wouldn't? . . . 'Cause . . . 'cause he woulda gone away an'
left me, that's why. So . . . so I jest . . . I jest kept fol-
lerin' him. . . . Needs me? He needs me, you think? Oh, I
wish I could believe that! If only once . . . I could feel
that! (*Sinks on the ground next to him—again clutching*
FLETCH.) Oh, Fletch . . . I'm so scared. I'm scared all the
time now. Every night when I'm waitin' for him to come
back . . . I pray for him, Fletch. . . . I believe, like my Ma
does, in havin' Faith. . . . (*Desperately.*) You're a smart
man, Fletch. . . . You *know* things. You been to college
. . . an' you know things. Matt'll listen to you, more'n he
will me. Talk to him when he comes back. . . . Tell him
he's wrong . . . goin' around with that gun . . . scarin'
people . . . takin' things that ain't his. (*Tears flooding her
eyes, her voice breaking.*) I . . . I love him . . . so terrible
much . . . an' . . . an' right now . . . I'm . . . so . . . so
scared!!! (*She puts her head against* FLETCH's *arm and cries,
deeply. . . . Frantically turning toward the entrance.*) Why
don't he come back? What's keepin' him now? He's never
been gone so long before. (*Beating her hands together, her
voice shrill. Rising crossing up center.*) Please . . . please,
somebody . . . somebody bring him back!

PATHS OF GLORY [1]

by

SIDNEY HOWARD

From the novel by Humphrey Cobb

GENERAL DE GUERVILLE *is Commander of the Fifteenth Army Corps. A gracious officer and a fine soldier, his appearance confirms the character—"decorous uniform, decorously worn, face clean-shaven and healthfully pink; eyes wise, kindly and steady."* GENERAL ASSOLANT, *commanding the Division is quite the opposite. Although a good Army man, his "the face of a man of action, of a man who would be satisfied only with a position of command . . . hard, aquiline, brutal, even." This meeting is held at Division Headquarters near the Front.*

Both men are standing at the salute, ASSOLANT *in front of the door by which he has just entered, the full light of the setting sun playing upon him. The older man's hand falls the first. Each gives the impression of sizing up the other.*

DE GUERVILLE. Shall we sit down?

ASSOLANT. Please keep my chair. (DE GUERVILLE *realizes how much the sunset light will help his appraisal of his new subordinate and seats himself therefore with his own back to the light. . . .*) I conclude that you have some unusual task for me. Since you'd give me no information by telephone. . . .

DE GUERVILLE. Aren't unusual tasks your special province, General?

ASSOLANT. Just now I'm more interested in rest than anything else.

DE GUERVILLE. Perhaps you read the dispatches in the Paris papers this morning?

ASSOLANT. I don't read dispatches, sir. I make them.

DE GUERVILLE. (*Amused.*) Of course! I'd forgotten that! (*He decides to ignore the impertinence.*) You know, at any rate, that General Headquarters has for some time been complaining about this sector.

ASSOLANT. (*Nodding.*) Hill Fifty-seven.

DE GUERVILLE. Called, I believe . . .

ASSOLANT. "The Pimple."

DE GUERVILLE. G.H.Q. have their own good reasons for wanting it captured.

ASSOLANT. They can't say you haven't tried.

DE GUERVILLE. My last effort failed yesterday.

ASSOLANT. I'm not surprised.

DE GUERVILLE. Unfortunately, this morning's dispatch reports a victory. (ASSOLANT *sits up, dangerous.*) And I'm turning to you . . .

ASSOLANT. I think I understand why, sir. I'm to take with my bayonets what a G.H.Q. ink-slinger has already captured at the point of his pen!

DE GUERVILLE. Oh, the dispatch has no bearing on . . . (*But* ASSOLANT *is on his feet in a fury.*)

ASSOLANT. I'm to watch the Paris papers, now, am I? And find my orders in the Paris papers! Well, General, my reputation as a fighting commander's secure enough to warrant my flat refusal to . . .

DE GUERVILLE. I was curious to see one of your famous outbursts. Now I've seen one, we've no time for further dramatics.

ASSOLANT. I apologize, sir.

DE GUERVILLE. You can take this hill if anyone can, Assolant. I'd have called on you first but you were busy at Souchez. Would you be good enough to sit down again? (ASSOLANT *complies.*) . . . I can give you all the artillery you want. . . . What I am about to say must be kept secret. Even from your Chief of Staff. Now this hill must be taken, General. To clear the way . . . (ASSOLANT *laughs, his harsh bark of a laugh.*)

ASSOLANT. Oho! An offensive coming! Is that it, General?

DE GUERVILLE. A complete break-through. You can see how hopeless that is till the way's been cleared. What an opportunity for the general who clears it! (*Then:*) This is to be an offensive to end the war. (*A wild burst of scornful laughter from* ASSOLANT.)

ASSOLANT. Are they still such fools they believe in that? Do you think we can afford another of those? End the war! End my division, you mean! (*A great weariness overcomes* DE GUERVILLE.) Let 'em give me fresh troops and I'll do it for 'em!

DE GUERVILLE. G.H.Q.'s keeping their fresh troops fresh. To take advantage of the way you clear . . .

ASSOLANT. Show me one good reason why I should walk into this trap. . . . (DE GUERVILLE *turns away. Then:*)

DE GUERVILLE. I'm authorized to promise an Army Corps to the man who walks in and comes out on the other side. (ASSOLANT'S *attention becomes exceedingly sharp.*)

ASSOLANT. What's that?

DE GUERVILLE. I've completed my errand here. (*He rises. But* ASSOLANT *begins to think better of things.*)

ASSOLANT. (*Low.*) It might be done. . . . Nothing's impossible. . . .

DE GUERVILLE. As I've said, you'll have all the artillery you want.

ASSOLANT. (*Kindling.*) That would be a new experience! And a free hand? You'd give me a free hand?

DE GUERVILLE. Of course. (ASSOLANT *is walking about the room.*)

ASSOLANT. Once an idea begins taking hold of you and you feel yourself warming to it . . .

DE GUERVILLE. That sounds more like it!

ASSOLANT. Oh, if they're set on this at G.H.Q.! . . . and I do take it on . . . (*He stops, staring at the shining insignia over* DE GUERVILLE'S *right lung.*)

DE GUERVILLE. Yes?

ASSOLANT. Would that mean that I might . . . that I might

hope to . . . That . . . (*He points involuntarily with the index finger of his left hand, while his right hand covers his own unadorned right lung.* DE GUERVILLE *looks down, understands, then:*)

DE GUERVILLE. (*With amused distaste.*) It might. It might easily. I believe I can assure you that it would.

ASSOLANT. I've never failed to take any position I promised to take.

DE GUERVILLE. I've never made any promise I didn't keep.

ASSOLANT. I'll take the Pimple. You'll have it for lunch day after tomorrow.

MEN MUST FIGHT [1]

by

REGINALD LAWRENCE AND S. K. LAUREN

EDWIN SEWARD *is Secretary of State. Coming from an old, aristocratic family, he is distinguished looking, kindly yet forceful.* LAURA, *his wife, is a beautiful woman. Her face still shows the marks of the tragedy she bore when her sweetheart was killed in the World War. She has a strong character. She is thoroughly alive and radiates her vitality. The* SEWARDS *have just returned from a long and supposedly successful trip to South America on a peace mission. The scene is their home in New York City in the spring of 1940.*

LAURA. (*Getting up.*) Ned—what's happened?

EDWIN. The worst thing possible. Down there.

LAURA. What is it?

EDWIN. Halsey has been shot!

LAURA. Shot—!

EDWIN. Killed! By some crazy revolutionist student. While

---

[1] Copyright, 1932, by Reginald Lawrence and S. K. Lauren; copyright, 1933, by Reginald Lawrence and S. K. Lauren.

he was on his way to present his apologies to their State Department.

LAURA. I—I don't believe it—

EDWIN. (*Crosses down to table.*) It's just been verified by direct wire to the White House. It'll be all over the country in a few minutes—all over the world—like wild fire!

LAURA. (*Stands for a moment, bereft of speech.*) The treaty—Ned?

EDWIN. Done for. . . .

LAURA. Done for—now—after all we've—

EDWIN. I know—I feel as badly about it as you do.

LAURA. Ned, I won't believe it's hopeless.

EDWIN. It's the worst possible thing that could have happened—

LAURA. What are you going to do?

EDWIN. Go to Washington at once— (*He rummages with nervous haste among the papers in his attaché case.*)

LAURA. I'm going with you—

EDWIN. No, please. I'd rather go through with this business alone.

LAURA. Ned— (*Goes to him.*) You're keeping something from me. What is it?

EDWIN. (*After a pause, firmly.*) We're sending the fleet down there at once.

LAURA. The fleet!

EDWIN. We've got to make a display of force. If they come across with the kind of apology we're going to ask, and if they agree instantly to certain pretty definite demands, there won't be any trouble.

LAURA. What demands?

EDWIN. It'll all be decided tonight. Simply to have them say, "Sorry, my mistake," won't be enough this time.

LAURA. They'll never agree to the kind of demands you'll make.

EDWIN. They'd better. (*Crosses down to table.*)

LAURA. They won't. They've got all of South America with them. And Japan. It means war!

EDWIN. Well—

LAURA. Have you committed yourself officially to this move— Sending down the fleet and—?

EDWIN. My opinion wasn't asked. It's the President's order.

LAURA. Are you going to obey?

EDWIN. I am. Because I agree with him.

LAURA. Ned!

EDWIN. (*Turning to her impatiently.*) Can't you see? Our national honor is involved.

LAURA. Is our honor staked on the life of a millionaire—?

EDWIN. He represents our country.

LAURA. He represents our millions. Must our boys be killed for that?

EDWIN. (*Impatiently.*) Listen, Laura. For three years those fellows down there have been itching for trouble. They hate us.

LAURA. (*Crosses to right of sofa.*) They have reason to.

EDWIN. For three years we've gone to ridiculous lengths to be nice to them. (*Crosses to her.*) Now the time has come to take them by the scruff of the neck and slap good sense and good manners into them—

LAURA. Ned—

EDWIN. (*Over center to her.*) I know exactly what you're going to say, Laura. And it won't do a bit of good. This thing has made me mad. Clear through. As it has every other right-thinking person.

LAURA. Right-thinking?

EDWIN. My mind is absolutely clear on what needs to be done. And I'm going to do it. And if I can't have your support, I must go through with it alone.

LAURA. It means war, Ned. War! (*They look at each other.*)

EDWIN. (*Crosses right to back of table.*) I must say goodbye to Maman. (*He starts for right door. She stops him.*)

LAURA. (*Over to him.*) Wait! Let me go with you. Let's stand together on this, as we have on all the rest. Let's fight with every weapon we've got against sending down the fleet—

EDWIN. Too late, Laura. If I opposed the President, I'd have to resign.

LAURA. Resign, then.

EDWIN. Oh—

LAURA. (*Following him.*) You're an important man, Ned. Speak up for peace—for sanity. Protest against sending down the fleet. Tell the country what it will mean. Let them drive you out of public life, if they want to— (*Through the open window can be heard faintly Newsboys shouting extra. Following* EDWIN.) You can make yourself a force, a great force to save us even now.

EDWIN. I can't follow you that far, Laura.

LAURA. (*Crosses to him.*) This is the test of your faith, Ned. The thing we've based our lives on—you and I. (*She grips him by the arm.*) Does that mean nothing at all to you?

EDWIN. I've done all one man can do for the cause of peace, Laura. I can't go any further and be true to what I feel is right and just and—manly—

LAURA. (*Crosses left to sofa. Spitting out the word.*) Manly!

EDWIN. I'm not obsessed by the fear that has haunted you all your life—

LAURA. Fear!

EDWIN. You've seen one war. You've seen it kill the man you loved, and since then you've been afraid of what it might do to your son! . . . (*He starts out; then goes to* LAURA, *his manner softening.*) Come on, Laura. See me to the car, will you? (*She makes no answer, but turns up to window. He looks at her a moment steadily and coldly, then turns.*) Well— Say goodbye to Maman for me, please. . . . (*He takes up his case and goes out. . . . The News-boys' shouts are now heard distinctly in the street. . . . She shuts it [the window] with a sharp, fierce gesture. Then crosses down to sofa and stops.*)

CURTAIN

THE FOOL [1]

by

CHANNING POLLOCK

"CLARE JEWETT *is* 28. *Smartly dressed, though in a fashion which suggests thought rather than expenditure, and pretty, in spite of a certain hardness."* She is engaged to marry DANIEL GILCHRIST, *assistant rector of a fashionable New York Church. He has aroused the antagonism of his parishioners by preaching on social problems that are contrary to the rich men's ideas. At college* GILCHRIST *was a football man and an ascetic; he is still in good condition. He is not the conventional reformer. He is humorous, honest and strong. "As yet his exaltation is in his smile. His great gift is charm— and sympathy."* It is Christmas eve. The scene is the chancel of the church.

CLARE. Got anything on your mind, Dan?

DANIEL. (*Quickly.*) What do you—

CLARE. I mean anything special to do?

DANIEL. Oh!—No.

CLARE. Take me home.

DANIEL. (*He beams.*) *I'm* getting *my* Christmas present early! (*Gets his hat.*)

CLARE. Where's your coat?

DANIEL. Outside. That is—I lent it to a friend. Oh, I've got another—somewhere!

CLARE. But you can't go out without a coat. (*Looks at wrist watch.*) Anyway, I told the taxi man to come back at half past four. That's the worst of not having a car. Well, we may as well sit down! (*He assists her, but his mind is afar.*) What's the matter with you, Dan?

DANIEL. Nothing important.

[1] Copyright, 1922, by Channing Pollock.

CLARE. There will be if you insist on going around without an overcoat! (*Looking at him narrowly.*) You're too generous. (*He is still afar.*) I say you're too generous! How are we going to be married if you go on giving things away?

DANIEL. (*Laughs.*) Is generosity a fault in a husband?

CLARE. That depends. Is it true you've been giving away—well—large sums of money?

DANIEL. Who told you that?

CLARE. A little bird. (*He laughs.*) And that you've refused to take part of your income?

DANIEL. Little bird tell you that?

CLARE. Yes.

DANIEL. Must have been a cuckoo!

CLARE. Is it true?

DANIEL. About the money? Yes.

CLARE. Why?

DANIEL. Well, there's the strike, and a good deal of unemployment, and I've got so much. Why—*I've got you!*

CLARE. (*Rises.*) Let's not talk about it now. (*She turns left; hesitates; looks at her wrist watch; looks off left.*) Yes; let's!—You're so changed. I hardly know you. We don't seem to want the same things any more.

DANIEL. What do *you* want, Clare?

CLARE. I want to be happy.

DANIEL. That's exactly what I want.

CLARE. How can anybody be happy without money?

DANIEL. How can anybody be happy *with* it? Anyway, do you think people are? Happier than the people who just have enough?

CLARE. In our day and age there's nothing worse than poverty! There's nothing more degrading than having to scrimp, and save and do without, and keep up appearances! I've tried it . . . ever since my father died . . . and I know! I can't do it any longer, and I won't!

DANIEL. Clare!

CLARE. (*She turns away and comes back somewhat calmer.*) I don't want to quarrel with you, Dan. I just want you to be sensible. . . . I love you, but I love the good things of life, too. I like to be warm and comfortable.

DANIEL. You can be sure of that.

CLARE. But that's only the beginning. I want good clothes, and furs, and my car, and money to spend when I like. I want my own house, and my own servants, and a husband who amounts to something. I'm no different from other women of my class.

DANIEL. I hoped you were.

CLARE. A year or two ago people thought you were going to be a Bishop. Today you've made an enemy of every influential man in the church. All that may be very noble, but I'm not noble, and I don't pretend to be. I don't feel any call to sacrifice myself for others, and I don't think you have any right to ask it.

DANIEL. I do ask it, Clare.

CLARE. You mean you're going on like this?

DANIEL. I mean I can't give you expensive clothes, and servants, and a big house while all about us people are hungry.

CLARE. What do you propose to give?

DANIEL. A chance to help.

CLARE. To help wash the dishes, I suppose, in a three-room flat in a side street!

DANIEL. And to visit the sick, and befriend the friendless.

CLARE. A charming prospect!

DANIEL. It really is, Clare. You don't know how happy we can be with work, and our modest plenty. There's so much to do—and they won't let me do it here. We've got to get *near* the people in trouble, and we can't with a big house and all that. I don't think we shall come to a three-room flat. (*He smiles.*) We'll have five or six rooms, and our books, and each other.

CLARE. I can't believe you're serious. You've always been a dreamer, but I can't believe you're going through with this fantastic nonsense!

DANIEL. I've chosen a narrow path, dear, but I hoped it might be wide enough for us both.

CLARE. It isn't. With your means and opportunities, you're offering me what any bank clerk would give his wife. I thought you loved me, but you're utterly selfish, and I think a little mad. You've a right to throw away your own life, but you've no right to throw mine. (*She hands him his ring.*) Our engagement is off. (*A pause. She starts for the door, and then hesitates, looks at her wrist watch, waits for him to call her back. When he doesn't she returns.*) Don't you think you're making a terrible mistake?

DANIEL. (*Looks up from the ring. Simply.*) No. (CLARE *turns again, this time quickly and with resolution, and exits left.*)

SPEAKING IN DIALECT

LET FREEDOM RING [1]

by

ALBERT BEIN

Based on Grace Lumpkin's novel

The MCCLURE'S *have always lived in the Carolina mountains. Jilted by a girl,* KIRK, *the eldest went down to the mill towns. Unable to make a living any longer in the mountains, the rest of the family have been forced down to the town to seek employment. Eight years later,* KIRK *now about 30, has grown into a tall, thin man with piercing, lively eyes, and a rapidity and grace which he has retained as his mountain heritage. He is explaining to his mother and brother why he became a union organizer.*

KIRK. (*Thoughtfully.*) Thar ain't no top, John. Don't fool yeerself like I nigh did into thinkin' so. Even if ye ris' as high as Mr. Wentworth—thar's still somebody with more power that ye must answer to. Ye'll alys be jest a spoke in a wheel—an' ye'll have t' grind down whatever the wheel hit chooses t' grind down, boy. . . . Awright—take a look at Basil right now—he's ris' with his own church an' a house an' he wint an' married a Strutt Street gal, I heerd . . . an' even if she ain't visited yore home—nor ye been invited t' thars—yeer proud o' Basil's rise, Mom—ain't ye? . . . But let Basil complain 'bout how the rest o' his mountain folk git along in this town jest once—an' the mill'll take his church an' his house—an' yes—even his Strutt Street gal right back from him. . . . (*In great earnestness as he rises.*)

I'm plenty bitter, Mom—an' so're many others I know an' have toiled among—men—women—an' even children—I'd like t' tell ye both why—. . . An' if I acted unlike a Mc-Clure, John, then ye must tell me after I'm thru if thar's still a man left among them. I mought have fergotten how one should act—but ye could have 'quired how I did 'thout condemnin' me aforehand. . . . (*Nods.*) Hit's true they ris' me t' be head foreman at Sandersville.—I ain't denyin' it—an' at a salary that kem t' forty-eight dollars every week, countin' over-time. . . . Shore, but I only collected the first weeks's pay, Mon.—I never collected no more. . . . There'd been a heap o' mishaps took place in the mill, an' the week I turned foreman two o' the women folk had their fingers crushed—a beam hauler lost an eye. Some o' the folks a-workin' in my shop kem t' me an' said, "Kirk, ye'll jest have t' take it up with the Super'tendent. Hit's onhuman t' let folk work at sech machines." But the Super'tendent when I seed him shugged his shoulders, sayin' "Cain't be helped— Let those a-bellyachin' look fer work somewhar's else—they ain't forced t' work here." I jest stood there rooted as he walked away, an' I didn't say a ward t' anyone. But three days later, when Tom Beggs that I'd worked beside fer years—when he got his hand ripped off t' the wrist right afore my very eyes—I saw red. I ran thru the mill, my dander arisin', an' I burst into the Super'tendent's office an' I blazed out at him that "By God, twaren't fair! Those machines have got t' be replaced. Hit's onhuman fer folk t' be a-workin' at 'em." He jumped up yellin' at me, "Go back an' tell the folk that the mill won't change a . . . machine." . . . Well, bedlam turned loose when I went back to the weave room—an' with me urgin' 'em on eighteen machines were yanked out and destroyed— And I gained nothin' by it. (*He chuckles.*) They rid me out o' Sandersville with a busted arm, an' both eyes swelled nigh shut an' no more foreman's job. An' Tom Beggs didn't git his hand back through my hotheadedness either— I have larned since how folks should go 'bout gittin' things righted. But I kin only ask ye both if any McClure

could know sech kenditions an' not have his blood bile with
bitterness and resentment.

STEVEDORE [1]

by

PAUL PETERS AND GEORGE SKLAR

LONNIE *is a young negro living in New Orleans. He is intelligent and sincere. Working for the Oceanic Stevedore
Company he resents the unfair treatment the negroes receive. He helps organize a union and is immediately framed
for a crime which the police have been unable to solve. It is
evening and his friends help him up from under the wharf
where he had been hiding all day.*

LONNIE. (*Stumbling.*) Sam! . . . Cold! . . . I feel like sleep-
ing, Sam. . . . I can't go no mo'. . . . (*Sits up.*) What's
dat? . . . Every time I hyear a noise, I think dar's someone
after me. Sam, Sam, if you knowed what was gwine on inside of me dis afternoon. Dey were gwine lynch me, Sam. . . .
Dem police drag me down de street and dat Mitch's gang
follow right after us, yelling, "Get dat nigger. Lynch dat
nigger. We make hamburger out of you, nigger." . . . I
don't know how I got away. We come to dat bridge, de mob
getting bigger and bigger, and I can't stand it no mo'. Somehow I break loose and jump right in de water. Dey shoot
after me, Sam. . . . Dey didn't hit me. Bullet don't get de
nigger. You got to lynch de nigger, burn him, burn him
alive. Oh, Sam, every black man dat was ever lynched, I
know how he feel, I know how he feel. . . . I can't rest,
Sam. All afternoon, crawling through dat mud. I could
hear everything on de wharf; de trucks rolling and de
winches grinding and de blocks squealing; all dem sounds
kept drumming in my ears: "Dat's where you belong, nig-

ger, down in de mud. De white boss, he belong on top. Get down, nigger, get down in de mud."

NED McCOBB'S DAUGHTER [1]

by

SIDNEY HOWARD

CARRIE *is the owner of a little restaurant in a small town on the Kennebec River in Maine. Her brother-in-law, whom she has never seen, has just introduced himself to her.* CARRIE *is "thirty, spare, handsome, humorous and amused. She never gives the impression of hurry and she is never idle. She realizes, without ever having given the matter a thought, that she is the equal of any man. She has had a hard time; few ups and many many downs, but her disasters have left her unscarred. She wants all she can get, materially, but she is unconscious of lacking anything mentally or spiritually."*

CARRIE. You ain't Babe? . . . Well, I certain am pleased to see you. Sit down. . . . Land sakes! Won't George be pleased t' see you, though! . . . There's the ferry startin' over now. . . . You see, my father's the captain of the ferry-boat—the *Governor Smith*—and George's fust mate. Bein' fust mate on a ferry-boat don't mean exactly the same's it does at sea. (BABE *says, "Oh?"*) Not on this ferry-boat, it don't. On this ferry-boat the fust mate collects the fares from the automobiles. . . . Oh, he's happy's a clam, George is. . . . Now he's jest fine. (*Sits left at table right.*) If I could only stop him from smokin', he wouldn't never cough at all. . . . It come on him from hevin' flu when he was in the Navy. . . . Well, I don't know's you'd call it exactly *in* the Navy, but he was in the Navy *Yard*. As a mechanic. At Charlestown. That's near Boston. That was where he took sick with the flu and pneumonia and like t' died in the hospital, and that was where we met, George and I. I won't never fergit how sick he looked, fust time I ever seen him. Come near breakin' my heart. I jest wanted t' set right down and care for him myself. Nursin' comes natural t' me anyway. You see, I was nursin' children at the time. In a private family in Boston. And I used t' go t' the hospital on my day off t' visit with a nurse there who's a friend of mine; used t' live here, up the road a piece. And she was George's nurse and that's how I met up with George and we got married. Kind of sad, ain't it?

ROADSIDE [1]

by

Lynn Riggs

HANNIE *is a buxom girl of 20. She is as free as air, boisterous, and jubilant. She and her father ramble about the old Indian Territory in Oklahoma in a covered wagon.* HANNIE *meets her equal when* TEXAS *swings down the road and stops at their camp. The scene is the courthouse at Verdigree where* TEXAS *has been brought for disturbing the peace. The* JUDGE, *outraged by the culprit's antics, hands his gavel to* HANNIE *and stalks out of the courtroom.*

HANNIE. Well, of all the— Whut's the matter 'th *that* ole mustard plaster? Whut'd he give me this here thing fer? Oh! That was the Jedge, wa'n't it? (*In high humor.*) Well, you heared whut he said! "Run this court yerself," didn't he? That ud be a good un! I'd do it right! I'd tear up the courtrooms and burn down the jails. I'd turn all the prisoners loose, let 'em run hog-wild. I'd give 'em money, I'd show 'em the road. That's the kinda jedgin' I'd do! (*She goes toward the* JUDGE's *stand.*) . . . I'd scalp all the guards, th'ow the marshals in the crick! . . . I'd burn all the law books, and start all over. I'd tell nobody whur to stand, and nobody ud tell me whur to set! . . . Mr. Texas. Now I'm gonna give you a little advice 'fore you start out of here to scalp the state of Texas again. . . . (HANNIE *comes down from the desk, slowly*.) Now then, you c'n do things fer yerself. I'm *th'ough* with *you*. I thought mebbe yer head wasn't quite as thick's a board. Now I know it's thick's the Rocky Mountains—and then some! You're as green as grass, and ignorant 's a blind goose in a thunderstorm. You don't know two whoops about women, and whut you *don't* know about *anything* would make thirty million books full of close printin'. When you first come along last night, I kinda tuck to you. . . . I thought you stepped right off a mountain some'eres. I thought you was full of shine like a scoured pot. I thought if you set, the sun ud set. Nen this mornin', when I heared you shootin' off yer head, I was mad as a settin' hen, fer about five minutes. When I ast you jist now if you was blind 's a bat, I mighta knowed the answer! *Course* you're blind as a bat—blind as forty-seven bats! If you wasn't, you'd see I've hotfooted it clear here to Verdigree, waded th'ough weeds and bresh and got chiggers on me. . . . And what fer? To try to git a fool of a man outa trouble that's had a landslide in his head, and cain't even remember who he's supposed to be! Now, git outa my way!

SUN-UP [1]

by

LULA VOLLMER

MRS. CAGLE *lives in the mountains of North Carolina. She is very outspoken, gruff yet kindly. Her only child,* RUFE, *is a likeable, sincere young man who has had a little—pain-*

[1] Copyright, 1924, by Brentano's Inc.; copyright, 1933, by Coward-McCann, Inc.

fully little—education at the mission school. America has en-
tered the war and he feels it his duty to go. MRS. CAGLE *is*
much opposed to this. She would like RUFE *to stay at home*
and settle his father's feud. The scene is the interior of their
cabin.

MRS. CAGLE *sweeping floor with brush broom.* RUFE *enters*
—puts hoe inside door.

RUFE. (*Wiping perspiration from his brow.*) Well, Mom,
the corn's all hoed. It won't need no more workin'.

MRS. CAGLE. (*Looking up.*) All right, Rufe. How 'bout the
tater patch? Put that hoe outside, son—

RUFE. (*Puts hoe outside door going to basin to wash his
hands.*) That's done, too. (*And washes his hands in basin.*)
'Tain't nothin' more to be done 'cept gatherin' the crap. Ye
don't have to worry 'bout that. I've done fixed it up with
Bud. He's goin' ter do it all.

MRS. CAGLE. (*Sweeping hearth.*) How much did ye agree to
pay him?

RUFE. I done paid him.

MRS. CAGLE. (*Stops sweeping.*) How?

RUFE. (*Going over and drying his hands on her apron.*)
With the money I've bin savin' fer my schoolin'.

MRS. CAGLE. I didn't want you to spend that, son.

RUFE. Well, I heared the Government wuz a goin' ter pay us
wages.

MRS. CAGLE. 'Tain't so.

RUFE. Maybe it is, Mom. If it is, I kin save that all the time
I'm gone, 'cose they say we won't need no money in France.

MRS. CAGLE. Whar IS France?

RUFE. I don't know. I heared it wuz 'bout forty miles
'tother side o' Asheville.

MRS. CAGLE. Goin' a mighty long ways to fight, seems ter me.

RUFE. Maybe it ain't so far. Think it wuz old man Todd
that told me.

MRS. CAGLE. I reckon he thinks he's been thar.

RUFE. (*Sitting down.*) I reckon.

MRS. CAGLE. (*Lays broom down, gets pan of green beans from cupboard. Sits on her chair and begins to string beans.*) Shore is a dry spell.

RUFE. Yes, 'tis. I hope it will stay dry, though, till I git to France. I allus hate to tramp in the mud. 'Spect them roads over thar air pretty bad.

MRS. CAGLE. Yes, I reckon.

RUFE. Mom, I've already fed the cow and the hogs. Sorter early, but I didn't want ter leave it fer ye. Bud said he'd milk fer ye tonight.

MRS. CAGLE. I ain't afeered o' work.

RUFE. I know ye ain't, but it's my place to do it. . . . (*Pause.*) Seems kind o' strange to think o' me gittin' married.

MRS. CAGLE. Ye do seem kinder young, Rufe. Don't seem more than yisterday that ye wuz a playin' 'round with mud pies. Times and children do change.

RUFE. Well, Mom, I want ye to know that if I married a hundred women—somehow—you'd always sorter be first in my mind.

MRS. CAGLE. Hit's only natural. I reckon if ye air old enough to fight, ye air old enough to git married. 'Pears to me like a man jest gittin' married ought ter stay at home with his wife.

RUFE. Mom, I hate to go off and leave ye feelin' like that 'bout my goin'. I wish ye could see it like I do. If ye cain't now, maybe ye will some day.

PORTRAYING CHARACTERS IN
UNUSUAL SITUATIONS

THE FIRST LEGION [1]

by

Emmet Lavery

The REV. JOSE MARIA SIERRA *is a Jesuit priest and a man of science. He is a Spaniard by birth. His dark hair and thin, pale face are the physical aspects of the mysticism which is a part of his character. Bedridden for several years from shell shock which paralyzed his legs, pneumonia now threatens the Father's life.*

The luminous, tremulous figure of the REV. JOSE MARIA SIERRA *appears on the landing stage right. A pale but shining figure, a shock of dark hair standing out against a cream colored dressing gown, he is almost an apostolic apparition. He sways uncertainly on his feet . . . and advances to railing on landing in shaky but triumphant steps.*

SIERRA. Deo gratias! Deo gratias! Oh God, most merciful: *Behold,* Thy servant walks! . . . (*Looking straight ahead from landing and oblivious of* FULTON *who is at piano beneath him.*) John—John—where is John? . . . (*Slowly.*) The doctor said—you wanted—to see me—suddenly I saw that I could walk—and I knew that I could come to you . . . are you in trouble, John? . . . (*Serenely.*) I have been walking with God, John. And I saw many things I could not see before. I saw myself talking to—*Blessed Joseph Martin!* . . . (*Happily.*) Blessed Joseph told me to get up and follow him—and so I did. And I came straight to you, John. Now I know the meaning of those words—I am the Resurrection and the Life. . . . (*Raising his hands in benedic-*

tion.) Benedictio Deo omnipotentis, patris et filii et spiritus sancti, descendit super te et maneat semper. Amen.

STRANGE ORCHESTRA [1]

by

RODNEY ACKLAND

JENNY LYNDON *lives with her family in a flat near Chelsea. They are impoverished artists and in order to defray expenses they take in lodgers.* JENNY *falls in love with one of them—an extremely handsome young man whom she believes is an artist. Just when the abscess behind* JENNY'S *eye breaks and she is blinded,* PETER *is caught running away with her manuscripts. Not daring to tell her the truth she is led to believe that he died in an accident. Her sister is with her in the following scene.*

JENNY. I must get used to the geography of this room. I walked round it three times yesterday without tripping once. Now, wait a minute. (*She moves forward but trips over a chair above table center.*) Oh . . . well, I could have done it. You must have moved the furniture, the chair wasn't there last night. . . . Did you type out the next chapter? . . . Do fish it out and let me feel it. . . . (*Walking round below table to left.*) Of course, you can't get the feel of it when you've taken it down from the beginning. It's definitely the best thing I've done, though. I know it is. No, don't go yet, darling, get it in a minute. . . . (JENNY *is now seated on the divan.*) If only being blind didn't make me feel like an irritating child. Esther, I wish everyone wouldn't be so suppressed about it. You make a pretence that I'm really the same as all of you. In a way you seem ashamed to admit that I'm blind to me. It makes it worse somehow. I feel if only everyone in the flat would congregate together

[1] Copyright, 1932, by Rodney Ackland.

with me there, and we were all to say "Blind, Blind, Blind" again and again, it would clear the atmosphere. . . . The same thing applies to Peter, too. I do so want someone to talk to me about him sometimes, but no one ever does. . . . I know (you do) but—I never quite feel your *mind* meeting mine. Is it because you're frightened it will upset me too violently? . . . It won't. Because I never really feel that Peter's dead at all. And I never shall feel it. I know now my blindness was providential. It's brought me so close to him. I know the real Peter, the Peter that I loved is as alive as you are, Esty. And if I wasn't blind, I'd never have realized that so clearly. Because, as far as I'm concerned, you're only a little more tangible than Peter is. You're only a presence and a voice. I feel Peter's presence just as clearly as yours, and I can see him clearer than you, Esty. Do you remember that line by Rupert Brooke? "And see, no longer blinded by our eyes." I wonder if Peter knew that poem. I hope death is like that, don't you, Esty? Esty dear, why don't you answer? Where are you? Esty? . . . What's the matter? You're crying, dear. Oh! Esty, don't! . . . You were crying about me, weren't you? . . . Well, don't, dear. It's awfully silly of you. I'm happy. I'm not minding the blindness so much as I thought I should. It's opening new things to me, exciting things. And I've still got Peter. And we're working very well, aren't we? . . . Well, all right, idiot. Now go and get the manuscript so that I can—feel it in my hands—and think how clever I am!

HOTEL UNIVERSE [1]

by

PHILIP BARRY

The scene is the terrace of a house in the South of France. It is early summer. The house was, at one time, the Hotel

[1] Copyright, 1930, by Philip Barry.

de l'Univers but it had been deserted for some years until ANN *took it. There were rumors that the house could, in the minds of the guests, resemble other places and people other people.* ANN *has brought her father there to live out the remainder of his life. He had been a well-known physicist, but he is an old man now, and considered a little mad. He seems to have some unnatural power over people even though he is not in their presence. A group of* ANN's *friends, among them* PAT, TOM *and* NORMAN, *are visiting her. It is their last evening. Though they are sorry to leave* ANN, *they are anxious to be away from this house that continually keeps them on edge and makes them think of their pasts.* PAT FARLEY, *the youngest of the men, is a goodlooking chap. A love affair, which ended tragically, has changed him from a clear-cut, happy boy to a cynical and morbid person.* TOM, *aged 40, though married, seems to be forever roaming the world searching for something, he does not know what.* NORMAN ROSE, *a handsome and successful Jewish banker, having worked all his life for the prominent position and recognition he has attained, is now unable to break his financial ties.*

TOM. (*After a pause.*) I unearthed a marble tablet in the lower garden today. It was in Latin and said: "To Semptronius who, at age 12, danced here and pleased." . . . (TOM *rises. All at once he is as excited as a child.*) I'd like to dance here, too. (*To* PAT.) Will you play? And would anyone mind? . . . (TOM *returns to the wall.*) Ten years ago I wouldn't even have asked. It's a rotten feeling, knowing your youth's gone—knowing that all the brave things you once dreamed of doing, somehow just won't get done.

PAT. (*As a small boy would say it.*) I wanna go out to the South Seas like Father Damien!

TOM. (*Soberly.*) I did, at that. . . . (*Reciting.*) Father Damien was a noble priest who went to the South Seas to help the lepers and got it himself . . . (*Suddenly* TOM *stands up upon the wall.*) Look, Mummy! Look where *I* am! . . .

(TOM *descends from the wall.*) Under the piano. (*He moves away from them, toward the table.*)—Under the apple tree— (*He seats himself cross-legged beside the table, whistling a tune softly through his teeth and trying to wrench the top from a wooden champagne-stick. A moment, then he calls as a small boy would.*) Hey, Pat! Pat! C'mon over! (PAT *comes forward to him.*)

PAT. Hello, Tom.

TOM. Hello, yourself.

PAT. Where's the other fellows?

TOM. How should I know? I got better things to do than follow *them* all over everywheres. (*He examines his stick with interest.* PAT *seats himself on the ground beside him.*) . . .

PAT.—Gosh, I feel good, don't you?

TOM. I feel all right.

PAT.—But don't you ever feel, Oh gosh, I don't know—*good?*

TOM. You don't feel very good when you've got things the matter with you, like I have.

PAT. What have you got? (*No answer.*) Aw, come on, Tom —is it really bad?

(TOM'S *head bends lower over his stick.*)

TOM. It's awful.

PAT. Aw gosh, I'm sorry—tell me, Tom—

(*A moment, then:*)

TOM. Will you promise never so long as you live—(PAT *nods eagerly.*)—I think I've got something, Pat.

PAT. What?

TOM. I think I got the leprosy.

PAT. (*Appalled.*) You've—? Gosh, Tom, why do you think that?

TOM. I read a book last night about Father Damien in the South Seas and he got the leprosy and I think I've got it.

PAT. How—how do you suppose you ever—

TOM. I gave an old woman a dime the other day, and she went and kissed my hand, and I think it must of been her that gave it to me.

PAT. But didn't you wash or anything?

TOM. I couldn't till I got home. And it takes awful fast. Look at that—(*He shows his wrist.*)

PAT. Where? (*He almost touches* TOM's *wrist—but draws his hand back fearfully.*)

TOM. Doesn't it look sort of—white to you?

PAT. It does, sort of.

TOM.—And scaly. That's the way it starts. My foot's the same way. I could tell for sure by putting it in hot water.

PAT. Hot water!

TOM. If you've got it, you don't feel anything, not even the water, even. Father Damien didn't. That's the way he knew. (NORMAN *is drawn over to them. He, too, has begun whistling softly. His tune is "Pony Boy."*)

PAT. Oh, he was prob'ly just a crazy ole priest.—H'lo, Norman.

(TOM *scowls.* NORMAN *gestures "Hello," and goes on whistling, hands in pockets.*)

TOM.—A *what*, did you say?

PAT. Well there *are* crazy priests. Anyways, I bet there have been, sometime.

TOM. Never. Never one. God wouldn't let there be.

NORMAN. What about Theo—philus?

TOM. Who?

NORMAN. Theo—philus.

TOM. What did he do that was so crazy?

NORMAN. Just burnt the library at Alexandria, that's all.

TOM. I never heard of it.

PAT. I did. Alexander the Great built it, quite a long time ago, to please his vanity.

NORMAN. (*Reciting.*)—And Theo-philus was a crazy Christian monk that burnt up the library which was the greatest in the whole world and which history tells us contained over seventy thousand volumes.

TOM. Well, if he did, I bet he had some good reason. . . .

NORMAN. He was crazy. . . .

TOM. Well, just let me tell *you:* when I grow up maybe *I'm* going to be a priest. See? Maybe I've got a vocation right this minute. See?

PAT. A what?

TOM. A vocation—a call.

(PAT *looks at him in wonder.*)

PAT. Gosh.

TOM. (*Closer to him.*) Just think that over, Mr. Fresh.—And when you hear of me going out to the South Seas and places like Father Dami—(*Awestruck, he remembered his malady. In fear he peers at his wrist again.*)

PAT. Is it any worse?

TOM. I—I think it's spread a little.

PAT. Listen—

TOM. What—

PAT. I know a fellow's got a doctor-book. Only he won't lend it. You got to look at it at his house. Shall we—?

TOM. All right. (*A moment. Then:*) Pat—

PAT. What?

TOM. What would you do if you had the—the you-know?

PAT. (*After thought.*) I'd kill myself.

TOM. You couldn't. . . .

PAT. Just the same I'd do it, though. I certainly wouldn't go around with the lepr—(TOM *claps his hand over his mouth.*) Let go!

TOM. You promised. (*To* NORMAN.)—You get out. Get out, now! If you know what's good for you—

(NORMAN *leaves them.* PAT *struggles.*)

PAT. Let go! I'm—I can't breathe. Let go—!

(*Still* TOM *holds him.* PAT *struggles harder. He begins to beat at him with his fists. Finally freeing himself, he goes at him more violently.* TOM *retaliates. They go up and down the terrace, advancing, retreating, clinching, separating, raining blows upon each other in dead earnest.*) . . .

NORMAN. (*Goes to* TOM.) Come on, now—that's enough! (*He holds his arm from behind.*) What's got into you two? . . .

(*They are gasping for breath, glaring at each other.* TOM

lurches forward once more. . . . PAT *suddenly slumps down
into a chair.*)
PAT. I'm—I don't know—(NORMAN *releases* TOM, *who stares
. . . at* PAT, *amazement growing in his eyes.*)

CHILDREN OF THE MOON [1]

by

MARTIN FLAVIN

JANE ATHERTON *is a lovely young girl endowed with charm
and grace. She is a serious person; her face is thoughtful;
her manner wistful. She loves the family home on the coast
of England where she lives a quiet and secluded life.* JANE
*and a young aviator are in love. To preclude their marriage
her jealous mother tells* JANE *that she is heir to the Atherton
taint of moon madness.* JUDGE ATHERTON, JANE'S *grandfather
led a full, happy and normal life previous to the time he was
afflicted by the family curse. His face is kindly and there is
no trace of sick room pallor. His hair is white. "His fingers
work restlessly, and his eyes glisten as his gaze shifts too
quickly from one thing to another."*

JANE *has resolved upon a course of action, but not upon
the means of its accomplishment. Her mind is dazed and
numb, and in addition, she is fearful of interruption. She
takes pains to make no noise, lest she acquaint* MADAM
ATHERTON *with her presence, and she watches the stair landing anxiously, expecting at any moment that her mother will
discover her absence and come in search of her. Amid all
these contending emotions, she seeks desperately to come to
a decision. She takes a few steps in one direction, a few steps
in another; and time and again she presses her hands to her
temples in a vain effort to control her thought. The con-
fusion of her mind, reflected in her face and movements,*

[1] Copyright, 1924, by Martin Flavin.

runs perhaps like this: "*Why did I come here?—I came to find him— I must see him— I must tell him— Yes, but what?—And where is he? Oh, where can he be?—I must tell him something.—What am I to do?—Oh, what am I to do?—Hark, was that a sound in the hall upstairs?—I must be quick— I must do something— Write— That's it, I can write.*" *She goes quickly to the desk, and stands looking down at it helplessly.* "*Yes, write—but what? What can I say? I must not make it hard for him— Oh, where is he now?*" *She brushes away the gathering tears, clenches her hands, and throws back her shoulders.* "*I cannot write— I cannot think of anything to say— Oh, if I could only see him—just for a moment—perhaps, perhaps it is not true— Wait, quick, let me see.*" *She goes to the door and holding the drapery close around her head, presses her face against the glass. In a moment, she reels back, shuddering and trembling.* "*I—I cannot think at all now. Look at my trembling hands—. . . . Like my grandfather's— My father's— My brother's— Like an Atherton's— It is true— It is true! I must do something now— It cannot wait— I could not endure all this again— Hark, is there someone at the library door?—I must write— Must write something.*" *She sits down at the desk, picks up the pen, and holds it for a long time poised over the paper.* "*I cannot seem to think of anything to say.*" *Her eye falls on the torn note she had started to write at her mother's dictation. She picks up the scraps and mechanically pieces them together.* "*What better than this?—It will be easiest for him— He will think me just a shallow little fool — He will quickly forget me— He will despise me— Oh, John, John, if you only knew.*" *She brushes away the tears again and with a great effort composes herself to copy the few lines. She reads what she has written, directs an envelope, encloses the note and seals it.* "*And, now what? This is the end—the end of everything.*" *A flood of grief comes now. She kisses the letter passionately, holds it to her breast; then spreads her arms out on the desk and putting down her head upon them, sobs silently but so convulsively that her whole body is shaken. Gradually the paroxysm wears itself out, and leaves her with a more calm and ordered mind. She rises from the desk and reaches for the bell pull by the door, then hesitates looking at the letter in her hand. "This final and irrevocable step— Must it be now? So soon— Wait— There was something else— I do not understand this thing — I need to know more— I meant to ask my grandfather— The letter— It can wait a little while— I shall give it to Thomas before I go back to my room." She puts it down on the desk, and with an air that is almost bravado, pulls back the draperies and throws open the doors. She leans against the door-post with her back to the Moon.* JUDGE ATHERTON *is sitting on his stool, his eye glued to his telescope. For a moment, she watches him, her hands clenched, her head held high.*

JANE. Grandfather! (*He does not heed her.*) Grandfather! (*He mutters with annoyance, motioning her away.*) Grandfather!

JUDGE. No, no.—Oh, it's you, Jane!—But I am busy, very busy, my child. Run away, dear, run away. . . . And—and close the doors; the light disturbs me.

JANE. I want you to tell me something.

JUDGE. (*Irritably.*) Some other time, Jane, some other time. (JANE *has placed herself that she avoids the direct sight of the Moon, and at the same time can watch the stairs.*)

JANE. I want you to tell me now. (*Something in her voice demands attention.*)

JUDGE. Now, Jane?

JANE. Yes, now.

JUDGE. Well, well, my child, what do you want? Be quick!

JANE. What is it that you see up there?

JUDGE. What do I see?

JANE. Yes. What do you see?

JUDGE. (*Tapping his head nervously.*) But you would not understand.

JANE. Perhaps I should, dear, if you would try to tell me. (*She kneels at his feet with her arms on his knees.*)

JUDGE. I talk with my friend, the Emperor of the Moon. He —he tells me things.

JANE. What does he say?

JUDGE. He—he tells me everything. He gives me news of your father, Jane, and of your brother, too. He tells me the secrets of eternal life, its joy and rest and peace.—He tells me what goes on upon the stars.—We children of the Moon, we know, we understand. (*His voice drones away.*)

JANE. Yes, dear, but listen! Look at me! (*She rouses him.*) You have not told me yet the thing I want to know. What is it that you see?

JUDGE. (*Shaking his head impatiently.*) No, no, Jane, you wouldn't understand.

JANE. Perhaps I should. I am an Atherton.

JUDGE. (*Excitedly.*) Yes, that is true; you are an Atherton. (*He takes her hands in his.*) I didn't think of that. You and I, Jane, we are Athertons; the only ones that are left now. Well, well, perhaps you should—perhaps you should—

JANE. Tell me.

JUDGE. Yes, I will try to tell you. (*He taps his forehead.*) I see— I see—

JANE. (*Eagerly.*) Yes?

JUDGE. But how am I to put it into words? These things are not the things of common sight. It is not what you look at with your eyes. . . . Life—that is what I see—patterns of color—pictures—pictures—

JANE. (*Spellbound.*) Tell me more.

JUDGE. But Jane, you are an Atherton. You can see these things as well as I.

JANE. (*Trembling.*) Do you think so?

JUDGE. I am certain of it, my child. (*He points to the telescope.*) But look for yourself.

JANE. (*Rising quickly to her feet. Passionately.*) Yes, let me look.

JUDGE. (*Greatly excited.*) You shall.—You shall. (*He jumps up and pushes the stool into place.*) There—sit there.—(*She sits down on the stool.*) And place your eye just there—the other one is closed—not tight against the brass, but so.—(*He moves her head.*) Now look, look close, and tell me what you see.

JANE. (*Faintly.*) I—I only see the moon.

JUDGE. No, no. Wait. Give it time. Watch close. The light is growing, spreading, is it not?

JANE. (*Breathlessly.*) Yes. Now I see it is.

JUDGE. Good! I knew that you would see.—Color is coming now—streamers of fire.

JANE. Glorious. I never dreamed such things could be.

JUDGE. (*Laughing crazily.*) Ah, it is true. You have the vision of an Atherton. But watch, watch close.—The ribbons lace and intertwine.

JANE. (*Ecstatically.*) Yes.—Yes.

JUDGE. What did I tell you?—But do not move your eye.—Far greater sights will come.

JANE. (*In a whisper.*) Life—it is life—eternal life—

JUDGE. (*Standing behind her, his hands on her shoulders.*) Hush, hush.—Just look.

FLOWERS OF THE FOREST [1]

by

JOHN VAN DRUTEN

LEONARD DOBIE, *in his middle twenties, is pale and emaciated looking. "He is eager, fierce, shy, ingenuous and resentful by turns. His accent is slightly common." Dying of tuberculosis and a complication in his brain he often has such severe headaches that during one he is unconscious of what he says or does. His talents lie in many directions.*

[1] Copyright, 1934, 1936, by John Van Druten.

Under the proper guidance he might be a genius. He works in a bookshop. During the past year he has spent his spare time doing research work on the war. His results have stirred him greatly and he has become an ardent pacifist. BERYL HODGSON *is about a year older than* LEONARD. *She loves him very deeply. She is an attractive girl of the lower middle-class. She is secretary to* NAOMI's *husband.* NAOMI JACKLIN *is about 40, although she doesn't look her age. When she was a girl* NAOMI *loved a young poet. During the war he became very disillusioned and in his bitterness he turned against* NAOMI. *At his death at the front he started a poem for her. Believing him delirious no one would write it down for him. The scene is the* JACKLIN's *sitting-room.* MR. JACKLIN *has been showing* LEONARD *some very fine pictures.*

LEONARD. (*Sitting chair center.*) I've had a marvellous time. It makes one think a bit, though.

NAOMI. Why?

LEONARD. Well, to think of the amount one doesn't know, stuff one's never seen. It seems as though there was so little time for all I want to do.

NAOMI. What do you want to do?

LEONARD. Well, first of all I want to travel. . . . That's only a beginning. But I've got to know what there *is*, first. I want to know everything that's *been* done . . . see all the things I only know from reproductions. That'd take a few years. After that, I might be ready to begin. . . . Only life seems so . . . short . . . especially when you've got to earn your living. (*Drinks.*)

BERYL. (*Rises and goes to him.*) Yes, and you've got to get up in the *morning* to do that. You'll be fit for nothing, if you don't go home.

LEONARD. (*Rising, suddenly enraged.*) Oh, leave me alone! Why do you always want to drag me away from everything? Hell of a lot I'm ever going to be able to do with *you* pulling at my coat tails all the time saying, "You're tired. You ought to go home." Well, suppose I *am* tired? Suppose I *have* got a headache? (BERYL *takes glass from him*.) Can't I decide whether I'd rather put up with it than go to bed? Oh, yes, and I know the doctor told me not to get excited—and I *am* getting excited—so you needn't tell me that, either. (*Subsiding as suddenly*.) I'm sorry. (*He puts his hand to his head*.) I'm sorry. Beryl's quite right. I ought to go home. I oughtn't to have come at all tonight, only . . . well . . . I did want to. I'm sorry, Bee.

BERYL. It's all right, Leonard. (*Puts glass down on table*.)

LEONARD. I ought to apologize to you, too, Mrs. Jacklin. Phew! (*He half staggers*.)

NAOMI. What is it? (*Rises*.)

LEONARD. Nothing. Just my head. Can I sit down a minute?

BERYL. Oh, Leonard . . . (*She goes to him and takes him to sofa*.) Is it bad?

LEONARD. Just for a minute. Oh! . . . ! (*He groans. Sits on sofa*.)

BERYL. Lie down, dear.

LEONARD. No, I can't. Not here.

BERYL. Mrs. Jacklin won't mind.

NAOMI. Of course not.

LEONARD. No, it's . . . I'm all . . . Oh! (*A fresh bout of pain*.) Well, just for a minute . . . if I may. It won't last long. (*He lies down on the couch*.)

BERYL. (*To* NAOMI.) Please . . . would you mind if I turned out the lights . . . or some of them? He can't stand it when he gets these pains.

NAOMI. Of course. I'll turn them all out. (NAOMI *does so. The stage is lit only by the firelight*.) . . . Isn't there something I can get you for him? Aspirin . . . Phenacetin . . . ?

BERYL. They don't do any good. It's just got to pass.

NAOMI. I'll go then.

BERYL. He shouldn't have got so excited. It was my fault. (NAOMI *goes out*. BERYL *kneels by the couch*.) How is it, darling? (*Sits on floor, back to audience*.)

LEONARD. Pretty bad. I . . . don't . . . don't talk. . . . I'm sorry I was rude, Bee.

BERYL. That doesn't matter, darling. That's all right. Please take my hand. Grip on to it.

LEONARD. No, it's better now. I . . . Oh! (*A worse bout of pain.*)

BERYL. Hold tight, dear. Don't be afraid of hurting. Darling, it won't last long. (*A shuddering groan escapes him.*) Is it *so* bad? . . . Why can't I help you? Why can't *I* have the pain. (*A silence. Enter* NAOMI *very quietly.*)

NAOMI. (*Almost whispering.*) How is he? (*Crosses left to sofa.*)

BERYL. Rather bad, I'm afraid.

NAOMI. I brought some eau de cologne.

BERYL. Oh, thank you.

NAOMI. Would you like to put it on his head?

LEONARD. Who's that?

BERYL. It's all right. (*To* NAOMI.) Would you mind doing it? He's got my hand. I don't want to leave go.

NAOMI. Of course. Mr. Jacklin is sending for our doctor. (*She bathes* LEONARD's *head, standing above the right end of the couch.*)

LEONARD. Who's that.

NAOMI. It's all right. You lie still.

LEONARD. Who is it?

NAOMI. Only me . . . Mrs. Jacklin.

LEONARD. Oh, I'm sorry, Mrs. Jacklin. I'll be better in a minute.

NAOMI. It's all right. Does that help?

LEONARD. Yes. Yes. It's cool. Don't go. (*He tries to sit up.*)

NAOMI. Don't get up.

LEONARD. I'm all right. Just a minute. Please, you needn't go. (*Pause.*) If only these guns would stop.

NAOMI. Guns?

LEONARD. Yes. In my head. They're fighting the war in my head. (*He gives a sudden cry, wrenching himself upright.*) There's someone being killed! Here! Hundreds of them. (*Grasping his head.*) Why can't they stop? Oh, why won't they stop? (*Then he slithers back again, half collapsed.*

There is a silence. NAOMI *moves over to chair right. Then from the couch comes* LEONARD's *voice but somehow different, emptied of personality.*) Is someone there?

BERYL. I'm here.

LEONARD. Please . . . someone . . .

BERYL. Darling, I'm here.

LEONARD. Someone . . . I want Naomi. Where are you, Naomi?

NAOMI. I'm here.

LEONARD. Naomi! Why aren't you here? Naomi, it's Dick.

NAOMI. (*By chair. Whispering in terror.*) Dick!

LEONARD. I want you, Naomi. I want to tell you . . . Naomi!

NAOMI. Dick!

LEONARD. Why is there no one here? I've got to write. Give me a pencil, someone. Nurse! Nurse, where are you? (*Sits up.*) What are all those boys doing here in bed? The whole ward's full of schoolboys. They've been hurt. They're crying out. They're dying! No, they're kids. You can't kill kids. There's a chap over there calling for Ann. Why don't you let him see her? Can't you stop that kid crying? I can't bear it.

BERYL. Leonard . . . Leonard . . . where are you?

NAOMI. Ssh!

LEONARD. That's right. They've taken him away. I want someone to write this down for me. It's a poem. Are you ready? "This my confession, having seen youth die . . . youth's exaltation die . . ." Oh, write it down, someone. I've got to get it written, and there's so little time. I've got to tell her. I've been so wrong, Naomi. We've all been so wrong. We said it was a job, our duty. Take this down. "This ghastly wrong we call our duty. Duty . . . beauty." No, our duty's not to kill . . . it's living . . . the best life we can make . . . only we kill each other, now, before we have a chance to learn. Dying for England . . . no, it's not enough! We're members of each other, the whole world. We're all on the same track, looking for knowledge how to live, that's all. Won't someone write it down?

"Youth's promise gone to waste. We kill our sons,
   Our heritage."
Our sons, Naomi. *Our* son. I must go on. Are you ready?
Oh, I can't remember it.
   "Their deaths we called their glory. We were lying.
   Their glory was in living, not in dying."
We've got to save them . . . keep them alive! . . . And
you, Naomi . . . you, my darling. I've loved you so, only
it all got twisted . . . spoiled . . . with all the hate around
me . . . turning our love to hate . . . the best and finest
thing in life turned into cruelty . . . in *me*. I don't think
even I . . . not even all the *world*'s hate . . . could kill that
love in *you*, my darling. . . .

NAOMI. Richard!

LEONARD. Please write it down! You, Naomi, you . . .
   "You against whom I sinned, denying life,
   Forgive me in your mercy when I cry
   Out of the darkness; 'It was Death, not I,
   The whole world's Will to Death, that drove the knife
   Into your heart, and laid our love to waste.
   I loved you always . . . always . . .'"
If I could only tell you that . . . Naomi, Naomi! (*He be-
gins to whimper, as though the seizure were coming to an
end, then falls forward,* BERYL *catching him in her arms.*)
Why . . . what . . . where . . . ? (*Then in his own
voice.*) Hello, Bee! (*He looks up.*) Oh, Mrs. Jacklin. Why
what's been happening? You were bathing my head. That's
the last I remember. I must have . . . gone right out. (*The
door opens and* LEWIS *comes in.*)

LEWIS. (*Quietly.*) The doctor's here.

(BERYL *and* LEONARD *go out, she leading him.*)

LEONARD. (*As they go.*) Was I out long?

BERYL. Just for a few minutes, that was all.

LEONARD. Oh, good. Last time it was nearly half an hour.
That shows I'm getting better, Bee.

LIST OF BOOKS

FROM WHICH SELECTIONS ARE
PUBLISHED IN THIS VOLUME

LIST OF BOOKS

FROM WHICH SELECTIONS ARE PUBLISHED IN THIS VOLUME

The Devil Passes, by Benn W. Levy. $2.00
The Road to Rome, by Robert Sherwood. 75¢
White Man, by Samson Raphaelson. $2.00
Jealousy, by Eugene Walter. 75¢
Ceiling Zero, by Frank Wead. 75¢
Call It a Day, by Dodie Smith. $1.50
Michael and Mary, by A. A. Milne. 75¢
Touchwood, by C. L. Anthony. $1.25
Art and Mrs. Bottle, by Benn W. Levy. 75¢
Winterset, by Maxwell Anderson. $2.50
Ethan Frome, by Owen Davis and Donald Davis. $2.50
Russet Mantle, by Lynn Riggs. $2.00
Blind Alley, by James Warwick. 75¢
Fly Away Home, by Dorothy Bennett and Irving White. 75¢
Family Affairs, by Gertrude Jennings. $1.25
Jewel Robbery, by Laszlo Fodor—adapted by Bert Bloch. 75¢
Hobson's Choice, by Harold Brighouse. 75¢
Spring Song, by Bella and Samuel Spewack. 75¢
Good Fairy, by Ferenc Molnar—adapted by Jane Hinton. $2.00
Parnell, by Elsie T. Schauffler. $1.50
Abraham Lincoln, by John Drinkwater. $1.50
Jayhawker, by Sinclair Lewis and Lloyd Lewis. $2.00
Victoria Regina, by Laurence Housman. $3.50
Brittle Heaven, by Vincent York and Frederick Pohl. $1.50
Lady Precious Stream, by S. I. Hsiung. $2.00

Pride and Prejudice, by Helen Jerome from Jane Austen's novel. 75¢

Brute Force, by Jacinto Benavente,—Eng. version by John Garrett Underhill. 75¢

Paths of Glory, by Sidney Howard from novel by Humphrey Cobb. 75¢

Men Must Fight, by Reginald Lawrence and S. K. Lauren. 75¢

The Fool, by Channing Pollock. 75¢

Let Freedom Ring, by Albert Bein from novel by Grace Lumpkin. $1.50

Stevedore, by Paul Peters and George Sklar. $2.00

Ned McCobb's Daughter, by Sidney Howard. 75¢

Roadside, by Lynn Riggs. $2.00

Sun-Up, by Lula Vollmer. $1.50

The First Legion, by Emmet Lavery. $1.50

Strange Orchestra, by Rodney Ackland. 75¢

Hotel Universe, by Philip Barry. $2.00

Children of the Moon, by Martin Flavin. 75¢

Flowers of the Forest, by John Van Druten. $1.50

NOT PUBLISHED:

Searching for the Sun, by Dan Totheroh